Think With Full Brain

Strengthen Logical Analysis, Invite Breakthrough Ideas, Level up Interpersonal Intelligence, and Unleash Your Brain's Full Potential

Som Bathla

www.sombathla.com

Your Free Gift

As a token of my thanks for taking out time to read my book, I would like to offer you a free gift:

Click Below and Download your **Free Report**

Learn 5 Mental Shifts To Turbo-Charge Your Performance In Every Area Of Your Life - in Next 30 Days!

You can also grab your FREE GIFT Report through this below URL:

https://sombathla.lpages.co/5mentalshifts_twf
b/

Table of Contents

Introduction

"One of the saddest experiences that can ever happen to a human being is to awaken gray-haired and wrinkled, near the close of a very unproductive career, to the fact that all through the past years, he has been using only a small part of himself."

—Orison Swett Marden

A Quick Story

One day, a professor entered his classroom and asked his students to prepare for a surprise exam. They all waited anxiously at their desks for the exam to begin.

The professor handed out the test papers to students with the text facing down. After he disseminated them all out, he asked the students to turn over the papers.

To everyone's surprise, there were no questions – just a black dot in the center of the paper. Obviously, the students were confused about how to deal with this surprise test. The professor, seeing the expression on everyone's faces, told them:

"I want you to write about what you see on the test paper."

The students were still confused, but they started on the mysterious task.

At the end of the class, the professor took all the answer sheets and started reading each one of them out loud in front of all the students. All of them, with no exception, defined the black dot – some tried to explain its position in the center of the sheet, while others described its size; a few others talked about the color of the dot. But every answer targeted the black dot.

After all the answers were read, the classroom was silent, waiting for the right answer to the confusing surprise test. Now the professor started to explain. He expressed:

"I'm not going to grade you on this; I just wanted to give you something to think about. No one wrote about the white part of the paper. Everyone focused on the black dot – and the same thing happens in our lives. We insist on focusing only on the black dot.

The black dot is an allegory; it represents the problems that you face in any area of your life, be they health issues, lack of money, a complicated relationship, or frustration caused by a stressful career. But we get so wrapped up in the black dot (our problems) that we miss out on the bigger context. By focusing too much on a problem, we often limit our thinking and are not able to seek out solutions that are readily available to us.

This is especially interesting when you consider how the black dot is tiny relative to the amount of white space it is surrounded by. If you start looking beyond the black dot and broaden your thinking to reflect on your problem (the black dot) in the context of the surrounding possibilities and solutions (the white space), you might start to get a glimpse of solutions in the form of resourceful people who may be able to assist you, opportunities in nearby areas, or skills that you may be overlooking due to your tunnel vision with regards to your problem.

And what is the moral of the story? The original message was that one should not only look at the dark side but also focus on the white space, i.e. the brighter side of the things. But as a thought experiment, I wondered what other lessons this story could offer, and, to my mind, this story perfectly addresses the concept of holistic thinking as well.

This anecdote also reminds me of the famous fictional character, Sherlock Holmes, created by Arthur Canon Doyle., who often proclaims this insight while investigating any complex case, **"people see but don't observe"**. You see the difference. While seeing is limiting oneself to only looking at the black dot, on the other hand, observing is equivalent to grasping the whole context of the black dot relative to the white space. Observing is analyzing the problem in its context by looking at the surrounding objects and people and examining the interrelation between them.

Now, let's depart the fictional universe and get into the real world. Our thinking is developed based on our routines and patterns, which are significantly influenced by our family background, our society, and the environment we spend most of our time in. In fact, our pattern of thinking and our perspective change heavily under the influence of the culture and geographies we belong to.

How Culture and Geography Changes the Way We Think

A few research studies have shown that East Asians are culturally more likely to explain any event or problem with reference to its context than Americans, who are focused solely on issues or problems in isolation. Two specific studies compare the context-sensitivity of Japanese and Americans and explain how thinking and behavior changes based on geography and culture.

Psychologists Richard E. Nisbett and Takahiko Masuda, from the University of Michigan, conducted an experiment,[1] wherein they presented a 20-second animated video of underwater scenes to two different groups comprising Japanese and American participants respectively. Afterward, participants were asked what they had seen.

Here is how both groups responded:

While the Americans mentioned larger, faster-moving, brightly-colored objects in the foreground (such as the big fish), the Japanese described more about what was going on in the background (for example, the small frog at the bottom left). Interestingly, it was also noted that the Japanese also spoke twicc as often as the Americans about the interdependencies between the objects in the front and the objects in the background. Japanese were more context-specific and viewed the whole event with a holistic approach.

Similarly, in another experiment, two groups, one American and one Japanese, were asked to take a picture of one individual. The results found that the American people frequently

[1]
https://sites.ualberta.ca/~tmasuda/index.files/Masuda&Nisbett2001.pdf

zoomed in on the picture in order to view the intricate facial features in greater detail. On the other hand, the Japanese, when asked to click a picture, frequently took pictures with wider coverage that showed the complete individual from head to toe, as well as objects surrounding that individual such as bookshelves, chairs, floors, etc.

One can readily see the similarities between both studies. The Americans focused on individual items isolated from their backgrounds and contexts, while the Asians gave more attention to the backgrounds and to the interaction or contextual relationship between these backgrounds and the central figures. Why do these two groups approach these situational experiments with such vastly different perspectives?

Erin Meyer, a professor at INSEAD, where she heads the executive education program on leading across borders and cultures, explains the reasoning behind it. She states that a traditional tenet of Western philosophies and religions is that you can remove an item from its environment and analyze it separately. Cultural theorists call this *specific thinking*. Chinese religions and philosophies, by contrast, have traditionally emphasized interdependencies and interconnectedness. The Ancient Chinese used the *holistic thinking* approach, believing that action always occurs in a field of forces. You can't disregard the environmental forces behind any action.

In fact, the Chinese have a concept of *yin* and *yang* in ancient Chinese philosophy that describes how seemingly opposite or contrary forces may actually be complementary, interconnected, and interdependent in the natural world, and how they may give rise to each other as they interrelate to one another.

Why did I start the book with these two studies?

I did not intend to compare any specific cultures or geographies or leave any positive or adverse comments on any specific set of the population. The idea is to simply communicate that when two people are dealing with or talking to each other in any context, in most cases, they make judgments about other people and label them right or wrong. They wrongly believe that the other person is not perceiving the information correctly. But what they miss out on is that there could be many perspectives or approaches of examining things, depending on their geography, culture, societal values, and upbringing.

What if you could understand all these perspectives while interacting with people? What if you could hear what they are saying in some particular context? What if you could also see what they are seeing?

Imagine, if you could, how different and exciting your life would be. It would be a journey full of exploration and adventure because every other person will show you their own perception or view about something that is different from what you think and believe. Every day, every meeting, and every interaction with another person will offer you diverse approaches of looking at things.

If that happens, you'll start making clear distinctions in your mind about why different people think differently and alter your perspective about things, places, situations, and people. You'll view things in a more holistic manner and offer better solutions.

Does that sound interesting?

That's what we will cover here: how to start thinking with your full brain.

Why Think with Your Full Brain?

Neuroscience has progressed enough, and there are many non-invasive brain-testing technologies these days like fMRI (functional magnetic resonance imaging) that can see inside of the human brain and have already figured out the inner constituents of our brain.

Robert Sperry's split-brain research that won him the Nobel Prize in medicine proved that the human brain has two hemispheres, right and left. Each side of the brain thinks in a different pattern. While the left side of the brain deals with rational and logical thought processes, the right side of the brain is inclined towards imagination, intuition, and interpersonal human aspects of thinking.

We are talking about thinking with our whole brains, so obviously, we will not get into a debate about which hemisphere is better or worse. The objective here is to use the full potential of your brain to make holistic and better decisions in most life situations.

In fact, people tend to use one side of their brains dominantly, just like people use one hand as their dominant hand while performing their regular tasks.

But you can't and shouldn't be solely relying on one particular segment of the brain to do all of your mental work. Let's set the research and proof aside for a moment and consider this statement with a logical perspective only. Why is a human being created with two brain hemispheres if they are not both useful and essential to one's life? Can you look at your outer body and say that any part of your body is inessential? Or can you just feel the sensations or vibrations inside your body and conclude that few organs of our inner system are inessential?

No body part or organ of your body is inessential. Every outside part or internal organ of the body has some role to play. So why would you prefer to use only one part or to restrict the usage of the other part of your most precious treasure – your brain? You should be using all the areas of the brain to their fullest potential...

Both hemispheres of our brain have specific roles to play, and we will examine these roles later in much greater detail. There is nothing bad about having a specific preference for one hemisphere or the other, but that shouldn't mean that you should be neglecting the other important aspects of your thinking brain. You can think with your entire brain capacity and still maintain a preference for one area of thinking, and that will make you a holistic thinker.

Neuroanatomist Jill Bolte Taylor describes the two hemispheres and how they work together in her book, *My Stroke of Insight*: "Although each of our cerebral hemispheres processes information in uniquely different ways, the two work intimately together when it comes to just about every action we take. **The more we understand about how our hemispheres work together to create our perception of reality, the more successful we will be**

in understanding the natural gifts of our own brains."

Here are a few of the benefits that you will reap from thinking with your full brain:

- **A heightened level of awareness**: You will appreciate everything that's going on around you with a holistic, context-based approach as your powers of perception and imagination increase.

- **Increased entrepreneurial capabilities**: Every business idea requires a lot of creative brainstorming. By thinking with your whole brain, you will be able to transform and integrate an idea (from its inception to actualization) into a business.

- **Faster progress in your career:** By understanding how different parts of your brain work, you will better understand the requirements of your clients, superiors, and organization, and you will be more equipped to meet or exceed their expectations.

- **Better relationships with family and friends**: Thinking with your whole brain enhances your interpersonal skills and emotional intelligence. This, in turn, increases your ability to understand the perspective of your family members, friends, or coworkers. Therefore, you avoid unnecessary arguments, are more open to others' perspectives, and consequently, you have deeper, more fulfilling relationships.

- **The development of multiple forms of intelligence**: Human beings are bestowed with multiple forms of intelligence that most people don't know about. We will cover them later on in this book. When you practice thinking with your whole brain, you become empowered to develop multiple types of intelligence.

Daniel Pink, the bestselling author of *The Whole New Mind*, has rightly said,

"Left brain approaches haven't become obsolete. They've become insufficient. What people need today isn't one side of the brain or the other, but ... a whole new mind."

What Should You Expect From This Book?

The title of this book, *Think with Full Brain,* is based on the premise that most people don't utilize their full brain potential. They employ limited aspects of their thinking abilities and, therefore, don't get the benefit of the ultimate level of self-actualization they are capable of.

I want people to unleash their fullest potential, and that's not possible until they understand their most complex organ: the brain. The objective of this book is to let the readers explore different parts of their brains and understand how thinking works differently in different parts of the brain. You'll learn and understand the dominant area of thinking preference in your brain, as well as where your blind spots are. Then we will explore how to enrich different parts of the brain and their thinking faculties to help you further strengthen your dominant way of thinking and make the other parts of your brain reasonably strong so that you can become situationally whole-brained and understand and handle different life situations in a wiser and more holistic manner.

By the end of this book, you'll realize a significant difference in how you see your own thinking from different aspects and use this knowledge to your advantage. Moreover, you'll also sharpen your brain to understand the other peoples' perspectives and thinking styles and adapt your thinking approach according to whatever situation that you are in.

Introduction: Key Takeaways

Our thinking preferences changes based on the cultural and geographical differences.

As per the studies described in this introduction, while Americans perceived people, places and situations more specifically and individually, the Japanese looked at the bigger picture, and they looked at people, places and things in the context of their surrounding objects and their interrelation with these objects.

Two types of thinking are **specific thinking or holistic thinking**, and these types of thinking are the result of two vastly different perspectives.

Thinking by **utilizing your brain's full potential offers multiple benefits**:

- A heightened level of awareness
- Increased entrepreneurial capabilities
- Faster progress in your career
- Better relationships with family and friends
- The development of multiple forms of intelligence

Thinking with full brain involves utilizing the full capacity of your brain as required in any given situation. The benefits of unleashing the full power of your cognitive abilities will help you to **improve your life in all areas, be** they financial or relational, and heighten your overall happiness.

Chapter 1: Why IQ Doesn't Solely Determine Your Thinking Abilities

****

"Almost all men are intelligent. It is method that they lack."

~ F. W. Nichol

Busting the "IQ Is Everything" Myth

Before we explore the anatomy of the brain more deeply, let's address one of the biggest myths that cripples many people and prevents them from starting to think differently. They believe that thinking smarter requires a higher Intelligence Quotient (IQ) and that a lower IQ renders them less capable of thinking in a holistic manner.

But this is primarily due to a lack of clear understanding of the concept of IQ.

To dispel this myth, let's briefly look at the origin of IQ tests. The original IQ tests were developed in the early 1900s, and their main objective was to help predict which children were most likely to experience difficulties in school.

An IQ is calculated by dividing an individual's mental age (measured by the test) by their actual age and multiplying the resulting quotient by 100. The resulting number is your IQ score, and it's compared to the rest of the population on a scale of 0–200.

While many tests have been developed since the IQ test's inception, such as the Wechsler Intelligence Scale for Children (WISC), the Stanford-Binet, Wechsler Adult Intelligence Scale Third Edition (WAIS-III), the Kaufman Assessment Battery for Children (KABC-II), etc., the major thing all IQ tests have in common is that they measure a person's cognitive ability — specifically, their ability to solve simple and theoretical problems.

Were you to examine the list of people with the highest IQs in the world, you wouldn't recognize many names. Many of the world's most intelligent and famous thinkers didn't have very high IQs. Albert Einstein and Stephen Hawking each had IQs of around 160, which is considered good but not astronomical. Their IQs pale in comparison to those of William James Sidis (an American mathematician who had an IQ score of 250-300) or Terence Tao, another mathematics genius (with an IQ score of 225-230).

Keith Stanovich, a professor of human development and applied psychology at the University of Toronto, Canada, and the author of *What Intelligence Tests Miss*, stated that **"IQ tests measure an important domain of cognitive functioning**, and they are moderately good at predicting academic and work success. **But they are incomplete.** They fall short of the full panoply of skills that would come under the rubric of 'good thinking'." IQ isn't everything.

"A high IQ is like height in a basketball player," says David Perkins, who studies thinking and reasoning skills at the Harvard Graduate School of Education in Cambridge, Massachusetts. "It is very important, all other things being equal. But all the other things aren't equal. There's a lot more to being a good basketball player than being tall, and there's a lot more to being a good thinker than having a high IQ."

Intelligent thinking **does not entirely depend on IQ; rather, it depends more on temperament and life-long learning,** as Warren Buffett and his billionaire partner, Charlie Munger, believed. You can outsmart people who are smarter than you if you have two skills, as Buffett and Munger stated in one interview:

a. Temperament is more important than IQ. You can work with a reasonable level of intelligence, but you need to have the right temperament.

b. Secondly, you must be committed to life-long learning. Warren Buffet is much better in his 80s than he was at a young age, as Charlie Munger has pointed out. If you keep learning all the time, it adds up, and you have a wonderful advantage over others.

In his book *Outliers: The Story of Success,* Malcolm Gladwell makes a solid case that people owe their success to a lot more than IQ. He offers convincing cases and arguments to show that above an IQ in the neighborhood of 110-115, IQ fails as a predictor of success in a career.

To put it differently, you need to be intelligent enough to handle the cognitive complexity of the information you need for a given role or job, be it law, medicine, engineering, accountancy or business. An IQ of around 115 is enough for that. But after reaching that threshold of "smart enough," your intellect makes little difference.

Let's Go Beyond IQ

Would you like to have an idea of how much IQ impacts your career success?

Howard Gardner, researcher and professor at Harvard University, states that assessing someone's intelligence through solely looking at their IQ level is a very restrictive approach. Gardner concluded, based on his review of workers' long-range data (from their early working years to the twilight of their careers) that **IQ predicts just 6 to 10 percent of career success**.

Therefore, we need to look beyond the theory of IQ and understand the concept of human intelligence in a broader sense.

Gardner defined intelligence as *"a **bio-psychological potential to process information** that can be **activated in a cultural setting** to **solve problems** or **create products** that are **of value** in a culture."*

To put it differently, intelligence is all about activating and utilizing your brain's potential and thus processing the outside information that empowers you to solve problems in a specific cultural environment by creating products or services that offer value to the world.

Therefore, Gardner developed the theory of multiple intelligences in late 1970 and first published this concept, in 1983, in his great book *Frames of Mind: The Theory of Multiple Intelligences*. This theory suggests that the traditional notion of intelligence, based on IQ testing that focuses on logical reasoning and linguistic abilities, is far too limited.

He explained in his multiple intelligences theory (also known as MI Theory) that different human beings possess different kinds of intelligence. He claimed that there were seven types of intelligence (some other experts claim way more than that, but Gardner stated that most of the intelligences could fit into any of the seven categories mentioned below):

1. **Logical-mathematical**: This type of intelligence helps people do things that require logic, abstraction, reasoning, numbers, and more critical thinking. A few examples of people enriched with this type of intelligence are Stephen Hawking, Isaac Newton, and Marie Curie.

2. **Verbal-linguistic**: People with high verbal-linguistic intelligence show great expertise in the fields of words and languages. Think of William Shakespeare, Emily Dickinson, and Jorge Luis Borges as perfect examples.

3. **Spatial-mechanical**: This form of intelligence helps people to more vividly visualize through their mind's eye and provides them with the necessary mental skills to solve the spatial

problems of navigation, to better visualize objects from different angles and positions in space, to more strongly recognize faces or scenes, and to notice fine details with enhanced ability. Examples of people with this form of intelligence are Michelangelo, Georgia O'Keeffe, and Buckminster Fuller.

4. **Musical**: Musical intelligence has to do with sensitivity to sounds, rhythms, tones, and music. People with a high musical intelligence normally have good pitch and may even have absolute pitch. They are able to sing, play musical instruments, and compose music. Mozart, George Gershwin, Ella Fitzgerald can be cited as embodiments of this type of intelligence.

5. **Bodily-kinesthetic**: This intelligence allows people to control body movements and gives them the ability to handle objects skillfully. It includes a sense of timing and a clear sense of physical action, along with the ability to train one's responses. One perfect example of this is Muhammad Ali.

6. **Interpersonal-social**: People possessing high interpersonal skills are characterized by a sensitivity to others' moods, feelings, temperaments, and

motivations, and the ability to cooperate in order to work as part of a group. Good examples of this intelligence are Nelson Mandela and Mahatma Gandhi.

7. **Intrapersonal (self-knowledge)**: People with this capacity are much better at introspection and self-reflection. They have a deep understanding of themselves, their strengths and weaknesses. They know what makes them unique and are able to predict their own reactions and emotions. Viktor Frankl, Thich Nhat Hanh, and Mother Teresa can be given as perfect examples of this form of intelligence.

Although the distinction between intelligences was explained by Gardner in detail, he opposes the idea of restricting learners to one specific type of intelligence. Gardner maintains that his theory should empower learners, not restrict them to one modality of learning. One can have many intelligences. Though there might be a dominance of one form of intelligence over the others, the idea is not to restrict the learning abilities of learners by some specific mode and rather expand it take the benefit of hidden intelligences. Gardner calls these different kinds of intelligences '**the human intellectual kit**".

Also, Daniel Goleman, bestselling author of *Emotional Intelligence*, has categorized different kinds of intelligence like emotional, social and ecological intelligence.

Another researcher on intelligence, Dr. Mindy Kornhaber, an associate professor at Penn State University, wrote a book titled *Multiple Intelligences*, in which she delved into greater detail regarding these multiple intelligences and how they improve the performance of students and adults equally.

She and her colleagues undertook the SUMIT (Schools Using Multiple Intelligences Theory) project. The research team studied a set of forty-two schools that had been using MI theory for at least three years. The results from these schools were very encouraging: 78% of the schools reported positive standardized test outcomes, and 5/8 of these schools attributed the improvement to practices inspired by the MI theory. 78% of the schools reported improved performances by students with learning difficulties. 80% of the schools reported improvement in parent participation, and 3/4 of these attributed the increase to the MI theory. Finally, 81% of the schools reported improvement in student discipline, and 2/3 of these attributed the improvement to the MI theory.

MI In Action

The multiple intelligence theory is being practically applied across locations and institutions to garner the benefits that it offers. A few examples are:

A theme park in Denmark called Explorama (http://www.danfossuniverse.com/) is developed on the concept of multiple intelligences. Explorama consists of several dozen games which individuals across the age spectrum can play. In the process of playing these games, individuals gain insight into the intelligences where they are strong and the intelligences which they should exercise more often. Also, one can predict how one will fare at the various play stations — this turns out to be a measure of intrapersonal intelligence.

Another application called Makey Makey (http://www.makeymakey.com/) gives individuals the opportunity to create experiences that draw on several intelligences. Informed observers can watch users at work and infer the nature of their intellectual profiles.

Thinking with Your Full Brain Entails Tapping Multiple Intelligences

Each of us is uniquely gifted with different types of intelligence. No one is given merely one form of intelligence. Though there could be one primarily or dominant intelligence, all of us are bestowed with multiple intelligences.

Thinking with full brain is built upon the key consideration that one must use everything that comes packaged in this wonderful gift: the brain. The problem occurs when we nurture only some limited parts of ourselves and build strength in those areas only because it happens at the cost of disregarding other aspects of our abilities.

I'm not saying that you shouldn't focus on your strengths or that you should not nurture any specific preference of thinking; rather, I'm suggesting that you should be situationally adaptable and use multiple faculties of your brain to optimally utilize your thinking potential.

For example, if you identify yourself as an introverted person and know that you can sit alone by yourself and come up with creative ideas, that doesn't mean that when you are out in social situations, you should be seen as a shy person. Of course, you won't be thriving in the crowd, but you also need to nurture your interpersonal skills.

I was listening to one interview by Robert Greene, an amazing author with many thought-provoking and bestselling books including *Mastery, 48 Laws of Power*, and his latest, *The Laws of Human Nature,* to name a few, when he talked about his daily routine or behavior with respect to his writing career.

He explained that when he would be in the research phase, he secluded himself from the world, as he wanted to do some independent thinking, build arguments, and arrive at conclusions for his book. But when the time arrived, i.e. the manuscript was handed over to the publisher for finalization and publishing, he would become as social as he could to support the marketing efforts of the publisher. He would attend as many TV appearances, podcast interviews, or other ways of exposing himself as much as he could.

You see, when writing and producing high-quality content, he was using his logical and verbal- linguistic skills, but he was also proficient in 'interpersonal intelligence' while interacting with the outside world.

Of course, we will discuss, at length, the constituents of thinking with your entire brain and how you should tap into different parts of your brain to become a whole-brained thinker.

How to Test Your Multiple Intelligences

There are many tests devised to test the multiple intelligences, but Gardner recommends one of the tests, known as the MIDAS (Multiple Intelligences Development

Assessment Scales) test, which was developed in 1987 by neuropsychologist Branton Shearer. This test typically gives a rough-and-ready sense of people's interests and preferences.

But Gardner also commented that such tests suffer from two deficiencies: 1) They don't actually measure strengths — you would need performance tasks to determine how musically intelligent, or spatially intelligent, or interpersonally intelligent a person is; 2) The tests assume that the person has good intrapersonal intelligence—that is, he or she knows himself well.

More than 20 years of the integration of the multiple intelligences theory into the career counselling process has proven that clients might obtain benefits from its application, such as the improvement of the career decision-making process and the enhancement of personal development[2].

This tool is stated to be very useful, but one must keep in mind that the results must be understood not as a label but as a starting point for future exploration. Labelling an

---

2

https://www.researchgate.net/publication/3090137
46_MIDAS--
_AN_USEFUL_TOOL_FOR_CAREER_COUNSELI
NG

individual based on this test inhibits their exploration into other areas of life, so this tool needs to be used carefully to assess one's current situation and then how to move forward from there.

While the MIDAS test above will cost you a few hundred dollars, here is something you can quickly do in the next 10 minutes and entirely for FREE to get some idea of your multiple intelligences. Click on the link to carry out this test: https://personalitymax.com/multiple-intelligences-test/

Your own understanding of different forms of intelligence and where you stand with respect to each such parameter will help you to understand the concept of thinking with full brain in the later sections of this book.

Now let's delve deeper into your head and understand its physical structure and a few concepts about your brain and the way that you think.

Chapter 1: Key Takeaways

Most people suffer from the misconception that our thinking abilities depend on our Intelligence Quotient (IQ). But in reality, IQ is a limited parameter of assessing cognitive functioning for academic and work success, but they are not complete.

The **general IQ Tests cover only logical-mathematical intelligences**, but there are multiple types of intelligence. Howard Gardner described **seven different types of intelligences** in his book (as listed below) that determine the success of any individual in different facets of one's life:

- Logical-mathematical
- Verbal-linguistic
- Spatial-mechanical
- Musical
- Bodily-kinesthetic
- Interpersonal-social
- Intrapersonal (self-knowledge)

There are many **tests to assess the level of your intelligence,** and one of them is the MIDAS test. You can also get a sense of your multiple intelligences through the 9-minute, 80-question test that was provided as a link in this chapter.

Finally, **thinking with full brain entails tapping into the multiple intelligences** of human beings instead of merely restricting your focus to logical or linguistic abilities.

Chapter 2: How Many Brains Do You Have?

****

"Knowing others is intelligence; knowing yourself is true wisdom. Mastering others is strength; mastering yourself is true power."

—Lao Tzu

It's an intriguing title, isn't it?

If someone had asked such a question only a hundred years ago, people would have already declared him or her mentally unfit and advised that he/she visit a psychiatrist. But today, with the evolution of neuroscience-based research and enough technological advancements, most people know what is inside the brain. Also, we briefly touched about this in the introduction.

In order to get a detailed perspective, let's look at some facts and studies related to the evolution of the human brain.

Before 1950, humanity's view was that the essential part of the brain was the left hemisphere, i.e. the same side of the body that housed the heart. Around the 1800s, there was evidence that it was only the left brain that understood the words and language that humans speak. The other hemisphere of the brain, i.e. the right brain, was considered to be retarded and instinctive, and it was widely regarded that it served its purpose in the primitive age, but with the technological advancements, it had outgrown its importance. And, therefore, according to scientists, the left brain was considered superior.

But it was only in the 1950s, when Roger Sperry, famous for split-brain research, discovered that the right brain is, in fact, the superior portion of the brain. He stated, "The so-called subordinate or minor hemisphere, which we had formerly supposed to be illiterate and mentally retarded and thought by some authorities to not even be conscious, was found to be, in fact, the superior cerebral member when it came to performing certain kinds of mental tasks."

Sperry concluded that the left brain was for thinking things through sequentially: it was more analysis-oriented and handled the words. On the other hand, the right brain was more for reasoning holistically, recognizing the patterns, and interpreting the emotions and non-verbal expressions.

Sperry was awarded the Nobel Prize for this research, and this transformed the way neuroscience and psychology started to view the mind and its internal operations. Not just an innovation by Robert Sperry, this technology had also been a game-changer in understanding the brain better during the past few decades. The invention of fMRI (function Magnetic Resonance Imaging) enabled man to track the movement and function of neurons inside the brain through scanning and imaging. fMRI displayed the evidence by showing the movement of the blood to some specific portions of the brain while performing different functions.

For example, if you were doing a complex mathematical problem, the scan would show the thick appearance of blood in the left hemisphere. On the other hand, while involved in some artistic work, watching some emotional movie, or letting your mind wander, the portions in the right hemisphere showed more blood cells providing the required energy to the brain.

In fact, the two hemispheres of the brain are specialized in a special way from a functional perspective.

A recent article in *The New York Times* cites research which suggests that emotion may be a right-hemispheric function. This notion is based on the finding that victims of right-hemispheric strokes are often comparatively untroubled about their incapacity, while those with strokes of the left hemisphere often suffer profound mental anguish.

Also, the two hemispheres are considered opposite to each other. In his great book titled *The Whole New Mind,* Daniel Pink explained some of the key differences in the functioning of the left brain and right brain:

- The left brain is analytical, i.e. it goes deeper into a specific problem and finds the reasoning behind the problem; the right brain synthesizes different pieces of information and looks at the bigger picture.

- The left brain specializes in looking at the texts and numbers; the right brain looks at the broader contexts in which the information is being presented.

- The left brain controls the right side of the body; the right brain controls the left side of the body.

- The left brain looks at things in a sequence, whereas the right brain looks at things simultaneously.

There has been a tendency to label people as left-brained or right-brained depending upon how they behave in their day-to-day functions. But this is a fixed-mindset kind of approach because, by such labelling, they convey a message to themselves to not try to use the other part of their brain. This silent inner belief cripples their ability to fully utilize their brain's full potential.

Also, opposite terms have been proposed to distinguish between the two hemispheric modes of "consciousness," for example: explicit versus implicit, verbal versus spatial, argument versus experience, intellectual versus intuitive, and analytic versus Gestalt.

Furthermore, in his book, *The Psychology of Consciousness*, Robert Ornstein, a research psychologist in California, refers to the **linear, left hemisphere as synonymous with lightness**, with thought processes that we know in an explicit sense. We can *articulate* them. He then **associates the right hemisphere with darkness**, with thought processes that are mysterious to many people but mostly to the western world.

Ornstein also points out how the esoteric psychologies of the East (Zen, Yoga, Sufism, and so on) have focused on right-hemispheric consciousness (for example, altering pulse rate through meditation). Whereas, in sharp contrast, Western psychology has been concerned almost exclusively with left-hemispheric consciousness, with logical thought. Ornstein suggests that we might find an important key to human consciousness in the right hemisphere. To quote him:

"Since these experiences 'transcendence of time, control of the nervous system, paranormal communication, and so on are, by their very mode of operation, not readily accessible to causal explanation or even to linguistic exploration, many have been tempted to ignore them or even to deny their existence. These traditional psychologies have been relegated to the 'esoteric' or the 'occult,' the realm of the mysterious — the word most often employed is 'mysticism.' "

Three-Part Structure of Our Brain:

While the two-part structure of the brain is more readily apparent to us from the perspective of the brain's physical structure and appearance, there is another perspective of looking inside the human brain.

In the 1960s, American psychologist and neuroscientist, Paul MacLean, invented the **Triune Brain Model** to explain the functioning of different parts of the brain in terms of its evolutionary process. According to this theory, **three distinct brains have emerged successively during evolution and now co-inhabit in the human skull.**

These three structures are often referred to as separate 'brains', due to the now-redundant belief that they operate independently (while in fact, they are simultaneously active in all circumstances). Those who subscribed to the triune brain model believed that the three major brain structures developed sequentially.

1. Reptilian (instinctual) brain

2. Mammalian or limbic (emotional) brain

3. Primate or neocortex (thinking) brain

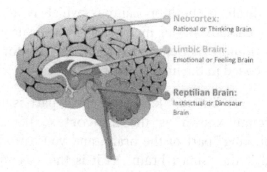

Neocortex:
Rational or Thinking Brain

Limbic Brain:
Emotional or Feeling Brain

Reptilian Brain:
Instinctual or Dinosaur Brain

The reptilian and mammalian parts of the brain are very basic in nature and the oldest in terms of evolution.

The **reptilian system** of the brain is responsible for the most basic survival functions, such as heart rate, breathing, body temperature, and orientation in space. This part of the brain handles all the body's involuntary functions and keeps you alive.

Coming to the next level of evolution, and also referred to as the "emotional brain", the **limbic system** is the reactive part of us that initiates the "fight or flight" response to danger. Our limbic brain contains the amygdala, which primarily deals with anxiety, sadness, and our response to fear.

The amygdala helps to safeguard us from danger and, in fact, helped us survive in the primitive age by promoting fight or flight in difficult situations. Another important part of the brain is the hippocampus, which is like a scratchboard of our memories – whenever you learn and experience anything new, memories get coded in the hippocampus.

And last but not least, the third part is the primate known as the **neocortex**. It's the "thinking" part of the brain, and you can also call it the "smart brain" as it is the executive part of our system. The neocortex is focused on higher functions, such as sensory perception, the generation of motor commands, spatial reasoning, conscious thought, and, in humans, language.

It's only this part of the brain that makes you distinct from animals, as it is responsible for human consciousness. The frontal lobe of your neocortex handles personality and reasoning, planning and executive functions. Most thinking happens in the front part of this frontal lobe called the **prefrontal cortex,** or the adult in your head.

The three various parts of the brain handle different tasks, but given modern, safe environments (we don't live in the jungles anymore), the role of the emotional brain is not often required; we don't feel the need for physical fight or flight in today's modern life. The reptilian brain will always be there to take care of our involuntary reactions (there is not much we need to do in that area) and the prime functions of our body like respiration, digestion, etc. that need to happen every moment of our lives.

Therefore, the most important part of the brain turns out to be the neocortex, which is responsible for success or failure, depending upon how you control it. The neocortex is literally the house of your thinking abilities, where you either don't do anything and let the older patterns dominate or you take control of this highly powerful human endowment and design your thinking to create the life you've always aspired to have.

The objective of this book is not to create a textbook explaining the biological or physical or evolutionary aspects of the brain. Rather, the above explanation of two-hemispherical physical aspects of our brain and the triune brain structure from the evolutionary perspective are presented here to give you some background before we get into the different aspects of thinking with our whole brains.

Let's now look at how thinking occurs in our brains.

How Thinking Works Inside the Brain

The human nervous system is responsible for the effective functioning of the internal organs as well as the outside physical activities needed to live life normally. But the most important function of the human brain is the cognitive work required for us to think about the outside world, analyze situations, and make the right decisions to solve our problems.

Life is all about finding solutions, and there are two ways that we can achieve this. One way is to choose one alternative from two or many options, so that we can make the choice that will provide us with the best possible value – also known as decision-making. The second way is to find solutions to problems without obvious existing alternatives through the process of generating many different alternatives – selecting the best option using this approach is problem-solving. Problem-solving is a holistic aspect of finding the solution to some problem; on the other hand, decision-making can be said the subset of problem-solving, where you must choose one out of the many alternatives available to you.

Before we talk about thinking with our whole brain, it's pertinent to understand how the process of thinking actually works.

Let's examine how our brains understand the multitude of information consistently bombarding them every moment of our lives. Neuroscience studies show that the human brain has more than 100 billion neurons. Each neuron has a cell body with two components: (1) a single long branch known as **axon;** and (2) multiple shorter branches known as **dendrites** (see image below).

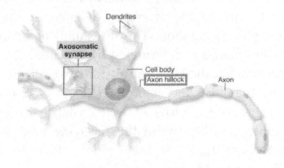

One important transaction that happens within the brain is when neurons pass on signals to the other neurons. They do it through touching other neurons, and that junction is called the *synapse*.

Current brain research supports the idea that **most learning and development happens in the brain through the strengthening and weakening of these *synaptic connections*.** There is some estimation that each neuron may have anywhere from one to ten thousand synaptic connections, and, therefore, the number of different patterns of possible connections in the brain is about forty quadrillion, a number that is beyond the comprehension of the average human being.

These neurons are the basic functional cells that appear to control our learning and thinking processes. They encode, store, and retrieve information as well as influence all aspects of human behavior. Neurons act like tiny batteries sending chemical and electrical signals that create processes to integrate and generate information. The threshold for firing at the synapse is determined by the number of chemicals (called neurotransmitters) released onto the receiving neurons (Bloom, Nelson, and Lazerson, 2001). At the synapse, these chemicals either excite the receiving neurons and cause them to fire, inhibit them from firing, or modify their excitability.

Examples of common neurotransmitters are dopamine and epinephrine, which are involved in affecting our emotions and mood.

Whenever we learn something new, that information is stored in the brain through the connection between different neurons. It is only through practice and repetition that we strengthen the connection between the neurons. In fact, neuroscientists have a cliché: ***Neurons that fire together wire together***. Apparently, all our learning and information occurs through the connection between the neurons. For example, imagine that a neuron that encodes a place and another that encodes an emotion are activated when a wrong experience is felt in this particular place. As a result of this experience, these two neurons fire together and then wire together. Then, whenever the neurons of this particular place are activated, the emotion is also retrieved. Small networks are connected with other small and large networks to resemble a forest of neuronal networks with tens of thousands of synaptic connections.

Therefore, it's important that we ensure that our neurons keep forming more and more synaptic connections. The more that we strengthen our neurons to fire with each other, the better our cognitive abilities will be.

When you take the foundation of your past experience (which is nothing but older synaptic connections) and allow this foundation to fuse with the newer concepts that you expose your mind to, you engage in the highest level of thinking, one that enables you to find the solutions to your problems.

In this chapter, we talked about the brain in terms of its structural aspects from a hemispherical perspective, as well as the theory of the evolutionary brain. And finally, we learned about how the neurons (the micro-elements of our brain) work inside the brain in order to facilitate the thinking activity.

This is an appropriate stage to examine the aspects of thinking with your full brain, as these concepts will build upon one another and present you with a different perspective of holistic thinking.

Let's move on to the next chapter and understand how to think holistically with our brains.

Chapter 2: Key Takeaways

Many different theories and research studies have been conducted about the brain's physical structure, but we can also examine the brain from an evolutionary perspective.

The **two-hemispherical left-right brain** concept was propounded by Robert Sperry and led him to win the Nobel Prize in medicine. While the left brain is more logical and rational, the right brain is more imaginative and instinctual.

In the 1960s, there was a study conducted by Paul Maclean; it looked at the brain from an evolutionary perspective and concluded that there are **three major brain structures** that have developed sequentially.

- Reptilian **(instinctual)** brain
- Mammalian or limbic (**emotional**) brain
- Primate or neocortex (**thinking**) brain

Regardless of whether we are looking at the physical structure or the evolutionary aspects of the brain, **thinking in the brain happens in a very complex and non-linear manner**.

Our brain is said to have 100 billion neurons, and all thinking is nothing but these different neurons firing with each other and making synaptic connections. These **synaptic connections form a neural pathway that determines our thinking preferences**.

Chapter 3: How to Think with Your Full Brain

****

"The goal is not to be a master of one or all styles, but to gain an awareness of all the styles so that you can honor your strengths and cultivate situational smartness in your areas of dullness."

~ Ned Herrmann

From a physical structure perspective, we have described the two hemispheres (left and right) of the brain. Furthermore, we have also examined (from an evolutionary perspective) the three different types of brains (reptilian, mammalian or limbic, and primate or neocortex).

Let's keep the momentum going. Now, what if we told you that our brains have four parts? This is not literally true; however, we can divide the brain into four parts from a functional perspective (explained later in greater detail).

But before we continue to divide our brains into further sections, let's understand a few more things. Though we already talked about different functions carried out in the left or right brain, that doesn't mean that neurons in our brains restrict themselves to specific hemispheres.

As you have just learned, our brain works through a powerful network of interactions between neurons through synaptic connections. That interaction doesn't happen exclusively on the left or the right side of the brain. A common misconception about the left and right brain is that our thinking preferences result from one single physical part of the brain being more connected, stronger, preferred, or more active.

But this is not the case. Thinking requires the activation of multiple specialized, complex networks that are shaped by experience and become stronger over time. Furthermore, these richly interconnected networks "learn" by adjusting the degree of interconnection: strengthening or pruning it over time as needed.

A great example of this is an unused skill that you might have developed at an earlier time in your life but have since completely stopped using. It might be a foreign language, a sports activity, or a work skill. When those areas cease to be used, and activity is directed elsewhere in the brain, they still remain, but they are not as strong as they might once have been.

When you reengage those areas, like picking up a musical instrument that you played years ago or a language that you have not spoken for a very long time, you can almost feel the struggle to reconnect those weaker links. If you practiced, over time, you could regain your acuity, but doing so would take effort and conscious mental activity.

Thinking in a particular manner is a matter of preference. The more that you use some specific part of your brain, the more dominant that part becomes.

Sadly, our world has always believed and spoken in terms of dichotomies like good/bad or right/wrong, and this approach has led us to coin terms like left/right-brained thinking. But it's not the optimal usage of our brain. Our brain is a cluster of neurons making interconnections with each other, and more synaptic connections these neurons make with other neurons, the better it is for us. A person with the highest amount of possible neuron connections enhances his level of understanding about the world. So the brain works as a whole, with both hemispheres of the brain working together.

Please keep the above in mind while we are now getting into a discussion about the four-part brain.

In the mid-1970s, Ned Herrmann, a psychologist and researcher at GE Management Development institute, Crotonville, proposed the concept of the four-part brain.

As per Herrmann, our brain naturally seeks patterns and organizes them. Through hundreds of millions of interconnections, the working brain provides pathways for specialized activities, which often involve many different areas of the brain, to take place. **Because of the way that the brain is designed, no specialized brain location ever works independently of the other locations; therefore, function becomes more important than location**. Placing the quadrants in the four positions helps people to understand the concepts and use them easily and quickly. Describing the brain in four parts is a metaphor to understand the preferred pattern of thinking.

Herrmann divided the brain into four different quadrants: A, B, C, and D:

- **Quadrant A: The Analyzer**. Logical thinking, analysis of facts, processing numbers.

- **Quadrant B: The Organizer.** Planning approaches, organizing facts, detailed review.
- **Quadrant C: The Personalizer.** Interpersonal, intuitive, expressive.
- **Quadrant D: The Strategizer.** Imaginative, big-picture thinking, conceptualizing.

The circular display in the image below represents the whole thinking brain, which is then divided into four conscious modes of thinking, each with its own set of behaviors.

(Image courtesy: Ned Herrmann Group)

Three Key Points

- Quadrants A and B are on the **left-hand side of the image,** and, as you can observe from their respective functions, are more related to the role played by our left brain. On the other hand, quadrants C and D are on the right side of the image, and the functions listed are more of an emotional and experimental nature, falling under the domain of the right hemisphere.

- Also, Herrmann assigned **different colors to each part to indicate the nature of the function**. Blue and green colors are more rational and organized, so they are used to represent the logical left brain. The color red is vibrant and often used to represent strong emotion, so quadrant C bears that color. And, finally, quadrant D is yellow to indicate elements of experimentation and freedom.

- Another way to look at is that **quadrants A and D are in the frontal portion of the brain**, which is responsible for executive memory, concentration and cognitive functions like thinking and analyzing. On the other hand, quadrants **B and C are in the limbic portion of the brain**, responsible for the sequential, step-by-step approach as well as the emotions and feelings responsible for interpersonal relationships.

Understanding the Individual Quadrants

Let's look at each of the four quadrants.

Most people don't typically think using each individual quadrant in isolation. The easiest way to get a sense of each quadrant's influence, as well as the relative compatibilities and incompatibilities among the preferences, is to examine each of them separately. Each of the following descriptions of the individual quadrants will help you to better understand and differentiate between them. As you read, you can start to think about which of these quadrants most apply to you.

Quadrant A

This quadrant handles activities such as analyzing, dissecting, figuring things out, solving problems logically, simplifying the complex, and getting facts. It relies on logic based on certain assumptions, combined with an ability to perceive, verbalize, and express things precisely. Quadrant A will calculate risk and won't move forward if it is excessively high. Argument is more important than personal experience, facts overshadow intuition, and emotion is to be avoided.

Quadrant A's ability to generalize from the specific and verbalize those generalizations make those who exhibit this thinking preference ideal technical problem solvers, but because they lack attention to emotion, they tend to appear cold, aloof, and arrogant. The solutions it offers, while logical, will often be impractical because they ignore the very real barriers, like dealing with human inertia or fixed attitudes. Its logic will chain the individual to the ground because he/she won't make the creative leap required to set out in a new direction.

The following words/phrases indicate the key characteristics of an individual exhibiting a quadrant A thinking preference:

- Focus
- Essence
- Precision
- Accuracy
- Clinical
- Factual memory
- Concrete
- Mathematical/financial
- Factual reasoning
- Performance-driven
- Logical
- Objective
- Diagnostic
- Analyzing (digging deeper)

- Quantitative
- Realistic
- Important to do it right
- Critical
- Rational

Quadrant B is very detailed, structured, solid, clear-cut, and down-to-earth. People with a thinking preference for this quadrant bear a number of similarities to those who have a thinking preference for quadrant A, but there are significant differences.

For quadrant B, efficiency is about making sure things are done on time and correctly, down to the last detail. There are no shortcuts. Quadrant A devises formulas, while quadrant B tests them. Quadrant B has little patience with or respect for the intellectual complexities that quadrant A finds so compelling. When you want to get things done, and when attention to detail is critical, the B quadrant is the go-to quadrant for sure. An individual using the quadrant B thinking preference will focus on one thing at a time and get it right the first time.

However, because quadrant B leaves little room for intuition, ambiguity, and emotion, others tend to view those who are exhibiting this thinking preference as controlling, small-minded, boring, insensitive, and antisocial. Its ultimate desire is for order and dependability and to preserve the tried and true, even though this may ultimately defeat progress.

The following words/phrases indicate the key characteristics of an individual exhibiting a quadrant B thinking preference:

- Organized/orderly
- Punctual/time-conscious
- Planned
- Structured
- Step-by-step approach
- Steadfast
- Sequential
- Thorough
- Security/safe-keeping
- Detail
- Traditional
- Drive/task-driven
- Neat
- Reliable
- Results-driven

Quadrant C is highly participative and team-oriented and considers people to be the most important aspect of life. When the mood of an individual or group changes, quadrant C is immediately aware of this and responsive to it. People with this thinking preference have little time for logic or theory. Experience is reality; achieving goals doesn't matter if they violate human processes, and personal satisfaction is the prime measure of success.

Because of his/her faith in groups and his/her openness to each person's contributions, an individual exhibiting a quadrant C preference tends to be viewed as agreeable, nice to have around, and supportive. But he/she can be undisciplined, overly sentimental, and sometimes impractical because he/she refuses to deal with facts, goals, time, and money. Most of what he/she talks about is hard to verbalize, so connection and flow become more important than content. The problem with those who exhibit a quadrant C thinking preference is that others can become frustrated by their unfocused, continual talk.

The following words/phrases indicate the key characteristics of an individual exhibiting a quadrant C thinking preference:

- Non-verbal cues
- Touch
- Cooperation
- Sociable (one-on-one and in groups)
- Take part
- Accessible
- Approachable
- Expressive
- Empathy
- Teamwork
- People focus

- Responsive
- Receptive
- Sensitive
- Support
- People awareness
- People perceptive
- Involved
- Playful
- Respectful

Quadrant D is intuitive, holistic, and adventurous. It takes risks, speaks in metaphors, and thrives on the excitement of new ideas, possibilities, variety, incongruities, and questions that sound obvious but actually go the heart of the matter.

Someone with a thinking preference for quadrant D tends to be a true visionary, in the best sense of the word, but often has trouble working with others because he/she is largely nonverbal and has difficulty explaining things or putting concepts into words. This quadrant lacks quadrant C's need to connect. So an individual exhibiting this thinking preference does not want to slow down to the speed that's necessary for everyone else to catch up or spend energy on developing structure. He/she dislikes structure, words, and logic because he/she feels that all of these get in the way of the flow of ideas and energy.

The following words/phrases indicate the key characteristics of an individual exhibiting a quadrant D thinking preference:

- Holistic/big picture
- Flexible
- Risk-taking
- Curious
- Looking for alternatives
- Experimentation
- Artistic
- Speculation
- Imaginative
- Strategic
- Simultaneous (doing many things at once)
- Fantasy
- Visualizing
- Synthesis (link ideas)
- Idea-intuition
- Investigation
- Integrating ideas
- Unstructured
- Preference for change

It's important to reiterate here that this four-part structure does not relate to specific locations in the brain; it is a metaphorical depiction model of four thinking preferences.

How can we clearly understand how such people look and behave? I liked the way that Herrmann elaborated on this by way of an example cited in his book, *The Whole Brain Business Book* (that I recommend reading) about four people with different thinking preferences working in an organization. The example shows that if you ask each of the four individuals a specific question about how to increase the organization's bottom line (profits), their answer will reveal the type of thinking preference they prefer. Let's understand the clear distinction through the example below:

Adrian is a finance manager in an organization. Though he is polite and courteous, he is more focused on business and tends toward a more directive side of the management. The human resources staff often gets complaints that Adrian's style is too hard, with an emphasis on the facts and too little attention to individuals' feelings. When asked the question, "What can we do to increase our bottom line?" He replies, "We need to upgrade our systems so we can increase our capacity, speed, and overall return on investment. Although we'll have to make an initial up-front investment, we'll be able to save time, reduce staff, and eliminate the overtime and additional employment expenses that are eating into our profits." He has data sets, calculations, and spreadsheets to back up his statements.

Brian is the manager in charge of production. For him, efficiency is paramount. His department follows a comprehensive manual of procedures that he himself developed. No deviation is permitted. Making sure that everything runs according to plan, safely, and on time is everything to him, so he tends to be impatient with ideas and methods that deviate from the norm. When asked, "What can we do to increase our bottom line?" he responds, "We need to stick with the basics—orderly, reliable processes that have been tested and proven to work. Holding everyone accountable for the documented schedule and procedures that we have in place is critical."

Carolina is the manager in charge of customer relationships and service. She helps customers with any questions, complaints, or requests. She says that her job isn't just about making sure that customers are satisfied; it's about making sure customers "feel loved". Those on her staff appreciate that she is a great listener, someone who's always willing to be a sounding board when they need advice or just want to vent, but sometimes they're not so clear about her specific goals and expectations. When asked, "What can we do to increase our bottom line?" she replies, "We need to engage our customers, as well as our employees, on a deeper level so that they will feel more connected to what we do and know how much that we value them. It may mean offering more freebies and perks, but the long-term payoff will be worth it."

Donald is the manager of creative services. He has a knack for thinking up very imaginative, almost unheard-of ideas, but the real reason that he is a leader is that he excels at anticipating important trends before anyone else does, and he is good at conceptualizing innovative promotion and marketing ideas that others can flesh out. Because he prefers to act on his gut instinct, he sometimes overlooks small but critical details. When asked, "What can we do to increase our bottom line?" he says, "We need to be more on the 'bleeding edge' of our industry if we want to stand out. What's the next big thing? We have to be there before the competition even thinks of it, and that means we can't keep getting bogged down by over-engineered processes and procedures."

Although the above example gives a sense of different people having a thinking preference or style, it also gives some indication about the thinking preference prevalent and needed for specific occupations. The research by Herrmann showed that **different occupations tend to incline towards specific thinking preferences** due to the nature of activities involved as described below:

- For example, professionals like doctors, engineers, lawyers, bankers, etc. would be more inclined towards a logical thinking preference (Quadrant A).

- The job profile of planners, bookkeepers, administrators, and supervisors requires more organizing and involves sequential thinking; hence, Quadrant B is their thinking preference.

- Quadrant C is interpersonal, so people who are teachers/trainers, musicians, salespeople or social workers most often fall into this category.

- And lastly, entrepreneurs, artists, strategists, etc. prefer to strategize and experiment with different concepts using high-level thinking, so they fit into the Quadrant D thinking preference style.

Preference Versus Competency

The central theme of Herrmann's whole-brain thinking model was that our preferences affect our choices. But our preferences are different from our competencies.

He stated that it's not that people are, by genetics, inclined towards one particular mode. In fact, you might have already observed that most children are primarily experimenters by nature and emotional beings. However, when they are growing up, they are taught and often rewarded for being more rational and practical. To be rational and logical is a safer and secure path, and it's well-trodden by many others in society, so there is a perception of low risk, and it's comforting, too.

However, all of us have all of the traits that are shown in the ABCD four-quadrant model; it's only the traits that we prefer the most that becomes dominant over a period of time.

The moot point here is that our **preference level does not correspond to our competence level.**

Perfection, in any particular field, comes from things or activities that attract you. Competence comes from training and experience. Therefore, true expertise and world-class competence can be achieved in our area of preference.

But here is the thing. Merely having an interest doesn't mean that you automatically develop skills and competency. Since your mind engages so well in those activities, this kind of work doesn't require an external reward, as the work itself is a reward. However, developing competency in areas of less preference requires more energy and effort.

"Applying Whole-Brain Thinking means being able to fully leverage one's own preferences, stretch to other styles when necessary, and adapt to and take

advantage of the preferences of those around you to improve performance and results."

~ Ned Herrmann

Why do we develop a preference for a specific type of thinking?

The more that you work to develop your skills in your area of preference, the more competent you will become in that area. When you become competent in one particular area of thinking, you deliver high value to other people, and people start to praise you for your work. This praise is a reward for your particular preference. If an action is rewarded often enough, it further cements your preference toward that particular approach.

Psychologists call this phenomenon a **preference praise loop.**

Moreover, the human mind is a pattern-searching machine. It's lazy; it examines past experiences and uses them to deal with current situations. This inhibits new thinking. Accordingly, our less-preferred thinking preferences become our blind spots, and then they impede growth in our lives.

Ned Herrmann developed a model known as the Herrmann Brain Dominance Instrument (HBDI): a questionnaire (with 120 questions) that provides a visual, easy–to–read picture of an individual's, pair's, team's, or organization's mental or thinking preferences.

Understanding different thinking preference profiles leads to a better understanding of the natural styles we use to process information. These styles impact our perception of the world as well as the way we approach problem-solving, the effectiveness of our interaction with others, and how we get things accomplished.

Preferences can be changed by choices in the same way as by volition because you are compelled to change your preference due to some uncontrollable outside circumstances. Here is a real-life example.

Herrmann cited an example about how his grandson, Karim, was able to change one of his preferences by practicing sufficiently. Karim was left-handed and was preparing for his SAT examination coming up in the next few weeks. But ironically, in one accident, he got his left hand so severely injured that he couldn't even hold a pen in his hand – so there was no question of writing anything.

Now, exams were just a few weeks away, and he was not able to hold a pen in his left hand.

Instead of dropping out of the SAT examination and postponing it for the next time, he chose a different approach. He started practicing with his non-dominant hand and put in an adequate number of hours practicing with his right hand. As a result, he could not only complete the SAT examination, but he also passed the test with a good grade.

The above example shows that with enough practice, you can change your preference.

In the above example, Karim had to shift his preference because of circumstances beyond his control; however, the objective of this book is to enable you to shift your thinking perspective voluntarily through your own free will. You don't need to wait for life to happen to make changes, because that's painful, as you *'have to'* adapt yourself forcefully. The better course of action is to *move forward* to change voluntary, have fun with challenges and master your mind in the process.

Male and Female Brain Physiology and Thinking Preferences Vary

Herrmann brought out one interesting aspect of brain research: there are differences in the physiology of the brains of males and females. For example, while the human male brain is larger (on average) than the average female brain, the neurons in the cortex of the female brain are packed closer together, and female brains possess more neurons than male brains.

There are other physiological differences that scientists are continually discovering, and Herrmann said that their research data consistently shows a difference in thinking preferences, with **males tilting more toward the A quadrant and females tilting more toward the C quadrant**. As per Herrmann's research, this data difference between the thinking preferences of males and females holds true around the world.

How does the combination of different thinking preferences work?

If you must deal with people who have different thinking preferences than you, that's a great opportunity for strengthening your overall perspective. Some thinking preferences work pretty well together, while a few thinking preference combinations clash with each other.

In a similar fashion, if an individual has two specific thinking preferences, the combination may help him or her in some cases, but it can be harmful in other cases. Let's examine this in greater detail. For example, if someone has a strong combination of A and B together, it will remind you of Captain Kirk of Star Trek.

If you have both a B and C preference, you are detail-oriented and people-oriented. Most HR people are like this; they will be detail-oriented as they have detailed rules and regulations and policy stuff for governing the HR function; at the same time, they need to take care of peoples' well-being. Again, it's a good combination of thinking preferences.

But unfortunately, if you try to combine B and D, it's like putting one foot on the accelerator and the other foot on the brakes. These two thinking preferences cancel each other out because the D preference will encourage an individual to always think of exploration and new ideas, but the B preference will require an individual to be certain of an outcome in all his/her actions.

When quadrants A and C are combined, people have internal conflict. While they make decisions based on the facts and details, they also feel guilty about hurting people's feelings.

———

In this chapter, we talked about four different types of thinking preferences to give you a holistic understanding of what drives different people to think and behave in a particular manner. You also learned that people develop certain types of thinking by preference and that the preference-praise loop strengthens that thinking preference.

Now onwards, in the coming chapters, we will cover the techniques and strategies that will help you understand how you can nurture these four different types of thinking preferences to become a situationally holistic thinker while boosting your key thinking preference as well. By following these strategies, you will further strengthen your key thinking preference, as well as understand and learn the other approaches that will help you deal with people of all thinking preferences and help you upgrade your problem-solving and decision-making skills.

Let's move on to the next chapter whenever you're ready.

Chapter 3: Key Takeaways

Our **brain is a powerful network of neurons** that interact with each other across the brain. A specific type of thinking doesn't result from any specific part of the brain; each individual has different thinking preferences. The more you use a specific part of the brain, the more dominant that part becomes.

Ned Herrmann propounded the concept of the **Four Quadrants of Thinking Preference** and advocated the view that different people have different types of thinking preferences. Here are the four Quadrants:

- **Quadrant A: The Analyzer**. Logical thinking, analysis of facts, processing numbers
- **Quadrant B: The Organizer.** Planning approaches, organizing facts, detailed review
- **Quadrant C: The Personalizer**. Interpersonal, intuitive, expressive
- **Quadrant D: The Strategizer.** Imaginative, big-picture thinking, conceptualizing

People choose to think in a particular way due to their preference, and it doesn't mean that they don't have the ability to think in a different manner; **preference is not the same as competency.**

Because of the **Preference-praise loop**, when people get praised for good work done in their area of preference, they develop that specific thinking preference further.

Understanding the different thinking patterns will help you deal with people of different thinking preferences and can **make you a situationally holistic thinker**.

Chapter 4: Effective Ways to Strengthen Your Logical Thinking Skills

****

"It is the mark of an educated mind to be able to entertain a thought without accepting it."

~Aristotle

To make decisions and solve the problems of this world, we need to understand how our thinking process works and how others think and perceive the situations they confront.

As Einstein once rightly said, we can't solve the problem with the same level of consciousness that created the problem. Therefore, the journey of human evolution is all about self-exploration and about how we think about ourselves and, accordingly, how we act and behave in the outside world.

You are now equipped with an understanding of how our thinking processes work biologically and how people can have different thinking preferences; you are already moving in the right direction toward becoming a holistic thinker.

Let's shift gears now and be more tactical and practical to develop our thinking in each of the quadrants one by one.

In this chapter, we will cover the ways to sharpen the front top left quadrant of your brain (quadrant A) and understand how you can improve your logical thinking abilities.

First things first. Let's understand the origin of the word 'logic'.

The word "logic" comes from the Greek word meaning "reason." The world definitely places a high value on people who display strong logical thinking or reasoning skills because their decision- making is based on factual data. In most cases, people don't want to make decisions influenced by emotions instead of facts.

Logical thinkers observe and analyze phenomena, reactions, and feedback and then draw conclusions based on that input. They can then justify their strategies, actions, and decisions based on the facts they gather. They don't go with their gut or develop a strategy because it "feels right". Logical thinking also requires setting aside assumptions and biases.

In his book, *Brain Building,* Dr. Karl Albrecht says that the basis of all logical thinking is a sequential thought. The process involves taking ideas, facts and conclusions involved in a problem and arranging them in a chainlike progression. To think logically is to think in steps.

Though people who exhibit this pattern of thinking may seem less playful and more serious, their process eliminates confusion and allows them to solve the complex problems of the modern world.

Everyone should use logical processes to arrive at sound conclusions. That's the reason that humans are bestowed with the precious gift of the mind: to observe, to analyze the situation, and synthesize the multiple types of information that are available to them before arriving at a conclusion.

This book is about thinking with your whole brain, and logical thinking is one of the most important components of it. You may have another thinking preference or dominant thinking style, but that doesn't mean that you should discount rational thinking or its importance in our daily lives.

Writing this book primarily requires an element of creativity because I'm pulling ideas from dozens, if not hundreds of places, and I am fusing them together to create an informative, creative product. Mine is a non-fiction book, but in the case of fictional work, it's a rather more spontaneous burst of creativity on paper, by way of the plotting of a novel and the depiction of the characters – the development of fiction is definitely a more creative process than that of non-fiction. But even creative works contain facts and need to be put together in a logical and organized manner.

Let me ask you the following question: Would you like to read a book that doesn't have a flow and one that doesn't sound logically appealing to your mind? Of course not; no one would be interested in the illogical product of a writer's disorganized imagination unless they are reading solely for entertainment purposes and willing to consume something that doesn't burden their mind (though some might argue that even an entertainment product requires some logic and rationale behind the content).

Therefore, logical thinking is essential. Let's now look at some effective techniques to develop logical thinking abilities.

EFFECTIVE WAYS TO IMPROVE LOGICAL THINKING

Get Rid of Your Confirmation Biases and Open Up Your Mind

The first and foremost requirement to develop logical thinking is to become open-minded – to think beyond your routine way of thinking and becoming receptive to hearing others' viewpoints on any situation.

We have many mental biases that make us think in a particular manner, and thus, we tend to miss out on the reality of a situation. Bias is nothing but a tendency to favor one thing over another.

Confirmation bias is known as the mother of all biases. Confirmation bias means that we have a very strong tendency to justify whatever we believe is right. In fact, we are always on the lookout for evidence to justify whatever we believe as the truth. Instead of learning something new, we listen with a sense of urgency to prove our point as correct. That's why Warren Buffet once wisely said,

"What the human being is best at doing is interpreting all new information so that their prior conclusions remain intact."

A psychological study was conducted with two groups of people: one in favor of the death penalty for deterring crime and the other against it. Both groups were provided with two detailed research papers on the effectiveness of the death penalty for deterring crime; one report established that the death penalty is effective, while the other concluded that it was not.

The results of the experiment showed that despite being aware of detailed scientific research and arguments and counter-arguments regarding the death penalty, each group became more convinced of the validity of their own position. People simply accepted the information that supported their preconceived notions and dismissed or neglected the conflicting information.

Why does this happen?

Chip Heath, the author of the book *Decisive,* aptly answers this as **"When people have the opportunity to collect information from the world, they are more likely to select the information that supports their pre-existing attitudes, beliefs, and actions."**

Also, one of the world's best-known skeptics and critical thinkers, Michael Shermer, author of *The Believing Brain,* has explained the reasoning behind why we are so cautious about protecting our beliefs. He says:

"We form our beliefs for a variety of subjective, personal, emotional, and psychological reasons in the context of environments created by family, friends, colleagues, culture, and society at large; after

forming our beliefs, we then defend, justify, and rationalize them with a host of intellectual reasons, cogent arguments, and rational explanations. Beliefs come first; explanations for beliefs follow."

It is our tendency to subconsciously decide what we want to do before we even figure out why we want to do it. We are naturally inclined to engage ourselves in the things we like rather than in the things we don't. Thus, we tend to find arguments for what we like and simply reject information that doesn't support these likings.

How to Get Rid of Confirmation Bias

You should actively look for the counter-argument for each argument.

Logical thinking is all about finding the rational basis behind the things. It's about asking the question of why something has happened or is happening one way and not another.

In this world, two people can have different opinions about the same things. To develop your logical thinking, you need to look at every aspect of the problem from multiple perspectives, including from a counter perspective.

Edward de Bono, the author of *How to Have a Beautiful Mind* and a proponent of lateral thinking, devised a formula called "six thinking hats" to explain how you can develop multi-perspective thinking. The six thinking hats formula allows you to analyze any problem from six different angles, so you don't miss any important aspects of the problem.

Let's look at an example. Four different people are standing near a building, but each on a different side of the building. Each one is given the task to describe the building's appearance, structure, and other details visible from their stationary location. After examining the building, the four people are required to meet each other and elaborate on the building, like the appearance, usage of glass, material, etc. Now it's obvious that all four people will have a different perspective on the building's appearance and, therefore, their descriptions will be unique to their own overview of the building. Therefore, each of them will have some difficulty in understanding the observations explained by the others.

Now, what's the best way to understand each other's perspectives?

The simplest solution is to make each person take one round of the building and have a look at the other three sides of the building one by one. Once each person has looked at the other sides of the building, they will be better able to understand the different perspectives on it.

The **six thinking hats principle is similar to looking at a particular problem from six different angles** before finalizing any solution to a given problem.

The colors of the six hats are **white, red, black, yellow, green, and blue**. Each hat represents a different perspective of looking at things as described below:

- **White Hat**: A white hat is like a white canvas. It means that you need to compile all the relevant information before arriving at any conclusion. Only then can you comment on any situation.

Two mathematicians, Edward B. Burger and Michael Starbird, in their book, *The 5 Elements of Effective Thinking*, give a wonderful piece of advice about achieving a deeper understanding of any situation or problem. They tell us:

*"Don't face complex issues head-on; **first, understand simple ideas deeply**. Clear the clutter and expose what is really important. Be brutally honest about what you know and don't know. Then see what's missing, identify the gaps, and fill them in. Let go of bias, prejudice, and preconceived notions. There are degrees to understanding (it's not just a yes-or-no proposition), and you can always heighten yours. **Rock-solid understanding is the foundation for success**."*

- **Red Hat**: Red color symbolizes warmth and emotions and requires you to look at the instinctual, intuitive or emotional side of the things.

- **Black Hat**: A black hat is for critical thinking and using your logic and judgment to find out what can be wrong in any situation. While wearing this hat, you should anticipate all of the possible negative outcomes that could occur in any situation.

- **Yellow Hat**: The yellow hat's role is the opposite of the black hat. This hat requires you to look at the brighter side; here, you look for value, benefits, and all the positive elements within any argument or alternative.

- **Green Hat**: The green thinking hat demands your creativity and offers ideas and suggestions for solving any problem.

- **Blue Hat**: Blue is the color of the sky, and you need to look at things from a big-picture perspective. The blue thinking hat plays the role of organizing the other various hats in your thinking process.

For example, if you would like to accept a job at a reputable organization, you must research all the arguments in favor of accepting the position. But at the same time, you must be willing to understand the logical and rational reasons why you might not want to do so.

When you listen to counter-arguments about any situations that you may come across on a regular basis, you develop a critical-thinking approach. One example of this method in action is the black hat strategy, as described by Edward De Bono.

Twentieth-century Danish physicist Niels Bohr, who made foundational contributions to understanding the atomic structure and quantum theory, for which he received the Nobel Prize in Physics in 1922, followed this counter-argument approach while experimenting with quantum mechanics.

In trying to decide whether quantum mechanics might be a correct description of our physical world, Bohr employed a practice of spending one day assuming that quantum mechanics was true and following the implications of that perspective, and then spending the next day assuming that quantum mechanics was false and following the consequences of that view. By alternating his views, he was able to explore each alternative more objectively.

This helped him to ascertain all the facets of that particular subject and broadened his thinking by questioning his own understanding and beliefs about any solutions.

Similarly, Hal Elrod, bestselling author of *The Miracle Morning,* described how he followed the same approach in one of his interviews. To finalize the objective views on any particular situation, he said that he would watch countless documentaries on that subject. He examines documentaries that support one point of view and then watches other documents that feature opposing arguments. If you look at things from a counter-perspective, you can make fine distinctions between various elements and there make decisions accordingly.

In fact, opening our minds to counter-intuitive ideas can be a way to discover novel solutions and build a deeper understanding of the subject. To deepen your understanding of a subject, try to consider it periodically from opposing points of view. For example, for one hour, you can research an argument, and for the next hour, you can research the counter-argument.

Have dinner with a person who has a different point of view and empathize with them. Try to build a new connection and new ideas from that person's point of view.

Attend conferences by multiple individuals on one subject to understand the topic from contrasting perspectives.

By developing the habit of looking at a subject from multiple perspectives, including a counter-perspective, you'll eliminate your own confirmation bias and more quickly develop logical and rational thinking methods.

The "Revolving Door Test" – Getting an Outsider's Perspective.

Intel's memory chip business started flourishing in the late 1960s after the company was founded, and it had almost had a monopoly in the memory chip market. However, in the late 1970s and early 1980s, its business took a hit due to the onslaught of Japanese companies entering the chip market with better quality chips; eventually, the Japanese companies started to grow their market share.

However, at the same time, a small entrepreneurial team of engineers had developed Intel's first microprocessor. In 1981, Intel persuaded IBM to choose this microprocessor to run their personal computers.

In 1985, there was an intense debate between Intel's executives about how to respond to the onslaught of Japanese competitors in the memory chip business. One day, Andy Grove, the President, and Gordon Moore, the CEO (who were the co-founders of Intel), were sitting in their office, and they felt dejected. Grove asked Moore what would happen if the company's management brought in a new CEO to boost the business of the company because they had been negatively impacted by the competition. He then asked what a new CEO could do to improve the situation. Moore, without hesitation, told Grove that the new CEO would get out of the memory business. Staring at Moore numbly, Grove said, "Then why don't you and I walk out of the door, come back, and do it ourselves?"

By asking what their successors would do, Grove and Moore were able to change course by altering their perspective of their company's situation. The approach that Andy Grove used was to **look at the situation from an outsider perspective.**

In fact, Intel's decision to stick with the memory chip business was motivated by a couple of illogical reasons. The amount that they had spent to compete with the Japanese companies was subconsciously viewed as a sunk cost (explained later). It was also a cognitive addiction, which is a mental bias where people stick to what they have been doing because it makes them feel comfortable.

How can we apply this situation to our practical life?

The reality is that when you experience a problem and want to make a decision about it, your decisions are influenced by your emotions. But you don't come across such emotions when you advise others in choosing similar decisions. This is because while advising your best friend, you would tend to objectively examine the situation and offer an unbiased opinion. You don't feel the emotions that your friend would experience in a particular situation and, therefore, your advice would be, to a large extent, objective and rational.

When you are indecisive about any situation, take an outsider's approach. Try to think about how you would look at the situation as a person who is not involved in it. Try to imagine what you would advise your best friend to do in such a scenario.

The outsider's approach will help you form an unbiased and unprejudiced view about the situation, and you can make your decisions faster this way. Such an approach provides you with solutions from an objective perspective, as if advice is received from an outside person who is unrelated to your problem.

Don't Make Decisions Based on Half-Baked Facts or Outer Appearances; Avoid the Halo Effect

The halo effect is the human tendency to make decisions without getting the necessary details and, therefore, making decisions based on oversimplified initial impressions. This is the phenomenon where, if you like someone due to a particular trait, you tend to believe that the person has other favorable qualities that they may not actually possess.

The word "halo" means a circle of light shown around the body or head of a saint or a holy person to signify their holiness. In psychological terms, the halo effect means that you form an overall perception of someone based on your judgment of one trait that the person possesses. It generally happens if you like someone; you start to assume that the person possesses multiple favorable characteristics and traits as well. This effect is clear evidence of a lack of critical-thinking skills, as when it occurs, you don't develop impressions of other individuals based on facts and evidence and may potentially make hasty judgments.

Psychologist Edward Thorndike first coined the term "**halo effect**." In the experiment described in his research papers, Thorndike asked commanding officers in the military to evaluate a variety of qualities in their subordinate soldiers. These characteristics included such things as leadership, physical appearance, intelligence, loyalty, and dependability. The goal of this experiment was to determine how ratings of one quality bled over to assessments of other characteristics. He found that high ratings of a particular quality correlated to high ratings of other characteristics, while negative ratings of a specific quality also led to lower ratings of other characteristics.

Practical observations of the halo effect are visible across many situations. For example, a teacher in the classroom can be subject to the halo effect in rating a well-behaved student as an intelligent, diligent, and smart person. In this example, the halo effect affects the student's overall rating and, in some cases, it can also affect the student's grade.

Similarly, in the corporate world, during employees' performance appraisals, the subordinates, who appear to follow the direction of their managers, enthusiastically get the benefit of the halo effect from their manager. In fact, the halo effect is probably the most common bias in performance appraisals. The supervisor may give prominence to a single characteristic of the employee, such as enthusiasm, and allow the entire evaluation to be colored by how he or she judges the employee on that one characteristic.

Therefore, the halo effect is misguiding you, and it is not helping you to make the right decision based on the holistic parameters.

What Should You Do to Avoid the Halo Effect?

The right approach to counter the halo effect is **to follow the objectivity approach**. To be specific, you need to list all the necessary parameters for arriving at a decision. Then you need to assign a weight to each parameter by assigning a specific number from 1 to 10 — 1 for the least weight and 10 for the maximum weight. Once done, you can make a total of all the parameters for the specific alternatives and then decide.

For example, suppose you have to hire an employee out of three candidates: A, B, and C. Here, you need to specifically list the job skills (including soft skills) that are necessary to perform the job. Your parameters can be qualifications, years of experience, industry work, confidence level, enthusiasm, the desire to learn, etc.

If you are not careful enough, the halo effect will start influencing your decision, because you might prefer one candidate over the other due to his/her attractiveness, communication skills, etc., which will tend to color your impression of his/her other traits, too. That's where being objective and giving weight to different parameters safeguards you from this biased approach germinating from the halo effect.

Don't Get Deluded Merely by Reasonableness and Authority

What everybody believes is not always what's actually true. Commonly held opinions are frequently just plain false. We, as humans, often get persuaded by authority and repetition rather than evidence and reality. If a statement is made by a person of authority, and if you keep hearing about certain things quite often, you tend to believe that statement as truth.

This is not a new phenomenon; rather, it's been around for centuries. In the year 340 BC, Aristotle asserted that objects fall at a rate proportionate to their weight – to put it simply, he said heavier objects fall faster than the lighter ones.

People accepted this for centuries because 1) it sounded reasonable, and (2) Aristotle, a person of authority, said it. This concept is known as **entrenched bias,** i.e. a combination of reasonableness and authority.

This thinking continued for nearly two thousand years until Galileo thought of challenging this thinking in the year 1588.

He went to the huge leaning tower of Pisa and threw two balls: one heavier iron cannon, and the other, lighter wooden ball of equal size. Surprisingly, except for the air resistance affecting the fall, both the balls fell at the same pace at the same point in time.

You see, thanks to entrenched bias, people continue to believe false assertions that can easily be disproven.

Therefore, to develop logical thinking skills, you need to question every assumption by seeking counter-arguments and experimenting with the other alternatives. You have to critically examine any assertion until it proves to be true according to the results of the test of objectivity.

Don't Perpetuate Your Mistakes Due to Sunk Cost Fallacy

One of our natural tendencies is to perpetuate the mistakes of the past. We tend to justify our past choices, even though we see evidence that they are no longer valid. People buy real estate or some other investment and come to the realization that it is a bad investment, but still, they continue to hold that investment in the hope that the market will correct and eventually make up for losses. But, unfortunately, even if the market continues to crumble, they still stay invested in their original decisions.

It's also called the **commitment effect**, where we stick to some decisions even when they are no longer working for us because we don't want to believe that our past investment of time and effort has been wasted or that the decision has become part of our identity.

Another example: people choose a specific career, and a few years later, they realize that they do not want to pursue it any further. But by that time, they have already invested so much time, effort, and energy that it becomes very hard to shift their careers. But the majority of the population continues to keep justifying their past decisions and doesn't take the necessary steps to correct them.

Why do they behave so?

This is because taking a new approach means admitting that our past decisions were wrong, and, frankly speaking, people are reluctant to admit to a mistake. Believing that we were stupid, careless, or lack the necessary skills hurts our ego.

For example, a manager finds it difficult to fire an underperforming employee because firing them would indicate that the manager had made a wrong hiring decision. So the manager continues to work with the underperforming employees, even though that decision compounds the other errors.

In the corporate world, if an organization shows a trend of imposing severe penalties for past mistakes, then employees don't change their courses of action and would rather perpetuate past decisions in the hope that the current situation will improve. Admitting mistakes could have dire consequences, so people choose to continue adhering to their past wrongs.

How can we avoid becoming trapped by the sunk cost fallacy?

From any organizational standpoint, if admitting to past mistakes would mean dire consequences, including the threat of losing their job for any employee, do you think anyone would stand up and admit their past mistakes? The answer is a clear NO; no one would take such a big risk.

But there are corporate cultures that have put in safeguards to prevent becoming trapped by the sunk cost fallacy. One such example is Amazon; they have spent billions of dollars, which they call "failure funds" on experimenting. They believe that they will only be able to come up with unique ideas from testing and experimenting and that those unique ideas will, at some point, pay for themselves.

"Failure and innovation are inseparable twins,"[3] says Jeff Bezos, Amazon Founder. "We all have that when we are little, but as we get older, somehow, it's not as cool to fail," Bezos said. "It looks clumsy. So we get in our grooves. We have a set of expertise and skills. It's kind of a comfort zone. But you have to constantly push yourself and say, 'no, I don't care about failure.'"

"At Amazon, we have to grow the size of our failures as the size of our company grows," he said. "We have to make bigger and bigger failures—otherwise, none of our failures will be needle-movers. It would be a very bad sign over the long run if Amazon wasn't making larger and larger failures. If you do that all along the way, that is going to protect you from ever having to make that big Hail Mary bet that you sometimes see companies make right before they fail or go out of existence."

Therefore, in order for an organization to thrive with new ideas, it needs to provide an environment where mistakes are not punished severely. The stakes may be high in some

---

[3] https://www.geekwire.com/2016/amazon-founder-jeff-bezos-offers-6-leadership-principles-change-mind-lot-embrace-failure-ditch-powerpoints/

situations, but organizations need to create low-stake islands in the high stake seas. It is by way of talking to mentors or trusted colleagues with whom people can talk about the things they don't know or need to improve upon.

On a personal front, where you are not accountable to anyone but yourself, it's you and you only who must have the courage to correct your past mistakes if they are not serving you anymore.

I have personally gone through phases where I had been justifying my sunk costs of time and efforts already invested in the corporate world to build a career. Obviously, after spending more than one-and-a-half decades in the corporate world in the legal profession, it was a temptation to continue with that career. But somehow, the drive to explore newer ways of living was stronger than continuing with my existing path, so I took a plunge to the world of entrepreneurship.

Therefore, don't get trapped in the past. Open up to experimenting with newer things; this will enhance your ability to logically examine all the pros and cons of all the alternatives and make the best decisions.

How Learning a Foreign Language Improves Logical Thinking

As an example, recent research has shown that people who speak a foreign language can reduce their inherent decision bias by thinking about the decision in the other language.

"A foreign language provides a distancing mechanism that moves people from the immediate intuitive system to a more deliberate mode of thinking," wrote Boaz Keysar, a professor of psychology at the University of Chicago. This forces the brain to move to a more logical and conscious process, thereby eliminating the frequently instinctive emotional decision bias.

You can create this same effect even if you don't speak a foreign language. Try stepping into the shoes of another role or another person whom you know. This intentional shift will engage your brain to better decipher the issue at hand from a different perspective and bring it to mind consciously. An easy technique is to visualize your living room and imagine what an interior designer might notice about it. Next, imagine what a thief might notice. How about a housekeeper or a real estate agent? This simple activity demonstrates how easily we can get in touch with other viewpoints. The mere process shifts our thinking.

Exercise Your Mind to Develop Logical Thinking

Treat your thinking abilities like any other muscle in your body. You can strengthen your body muscles by exercise and strength training; you can also make your mind sharper by doing brain exercises. Here are some quick ways that you can start sharpening your brain's memory and cognitive abilities.

- **Test your recall or memory.**

One of the best ways to sharpen your brain is to test your recall abilities. Test your memory by trying to memorize small things like a small grocery list or any series of words or numbers and try to recall it after some time. Read some paragraph or passage of a poem and memorize it. Try and see if you recall it after one hour.

- **Train your brain.**

The benefit of crossword puzzles on the mind is well-documented. Crossword puzzles force you to push your brain slightly beyond its capabilities, which causes the regrowth of brain neurons. This increases your overall brain power and can promote more sound and logical thinking. Pick up a crossword puzzle book from a local bookstore or do your local newspaper's crossword each morning. Also, playing Sudoku is another way to exercise your brain.

If you want to use your smartphone wisely instead of getting trapped into entertainment or social media apps, there are many brain-training apps these days that can help you to sharpen your thinking abilities. You can try using apps like Lumosity, Peak or Elevate for free in both android and IOS versions.

- **Learn a new talent.**

Learning anything new requires logic. Whether you want to learn to play the guitar, piano, or to learn any foreign language, this requires the application of a lot of logical thinking. By devising strategies that help you learn to undertake challenging tasks, you use logic and strategy to acquire new skills. Try taking up some of the following activities to boost your logical thinking skills:

- Learn to play instruments.
- Learn to draw or paint.
- Learn to speak a foreign language.
- Learn to cook.

- **Change up your routine often.**

Offering some different approaches to doing things offers a dose of novelty to your brain. Novelty helps the brain stay sharp and increases your memory. Try taking a different route to work than usual or cooking a new type of food for dinner than you typically would. Experiencing new things helps the brain stay active, which can help you to become a more logical thinker.

- **Engage in healthy debates.**

To improve your logical thinking abilities, you need to expose your mind to varying sets of information, as you learned in multi-perspective thinking. One of the best ways to do it to engage in healthy debates with your friends or family on some topic of common interest, which they are also keen to explore.

A debate does the multipurpose work of enhancing your thinking skills in the moment, as you have to process your thoughts in a cohesive manner to build an argument to present to the next person. This gives your mind exercise to think and improves your communication abilities and presentation skills while conveying your views to the other person.

Chapter 4: Key Takeaways

Logical thinkers **observe and analyze phenomena, reactions, and feedback, and then draw conclusions** based on that input. They can justify their strategies, actions, and decisions based on the facts they gather.

You can develop your logical thinking abilities by following the effective strategies listed below:

- Learn to **get rid of your confirmation bias** and become open-minded. Follow multi-perspective thinking and review the counter-argument for every assumption. Look at a variety of opposing views about any specific situation, as that will empower you to make fine distinctions and help you improve your rational thinking.

- Get an **outsider's perspective** in difficult situations. Learn how an outsider will observe any specific situation; follow the "Revolving Door Test".

- **Understand the Halo Effect**: Don't make your decisions based on incomplete information or just outer appearances.

- **Don't believe something because it sounds reasonable and because it's said by some person of authority**. Examine all assumptions critically on your own before arriving at any conclusions or decisions.

- **Avoid becoming trapped by the sunk cost fallacy**: Don't justify your past mistakes and don't continue to make the same ones merely because it is what you have done in the past. Learn from the past and move forward.

- **Learn a foreign language** to look at things from a different perspective and get rid of the emotional bias associated with your own language.

- **Exercise your mind** by using memory-recall techniques. Do brain trainings; switch up your routine activities and engage in healthy debates with individuals who have a different viewpoint than yours on any given topic.

Chapter 5: How to Organize Your Thinking to Get Things Done

****

"For every minute spent organizing, an hour is earned."

~Benjamin Franklin

As the name suggests, organized or sequential thinking is of the utmost importance when you want to get things done with the utmost precision. Organized thinking enables you to make plans, structures, and set up clear processes for taking all the steps needed to attain the desired action.

If you are already inclined toward this preference of thinking, you know how satisfying it is to see the clear structures, steps and processes for getting things done the right way the first time. You know that you can't run any mechanical plant, factory, or any other well-defined system unless you have clear standard operating procedures or processes to carry out different activities for manufacturing any product with particular standards or for operating any other system.

Those who have the least preference for this type of thinking may spend all of their efforts to avoid it. But they need to understand that this thinking preference can't be ignored entirely, as this type of thinking actually gets the things done at the ground level. Regardless of the amount of breakthrough creative ideas you have or the amount of logical analysis you have done in any situation, nothing moves the needle until you test and execute those plans at the ground level. And that's where the rubber hits the road; that's where you come to know the real challenges or problems that need resolution to move forward. Organized thinkers plan out a step-by-step system that provides the certainty of a positive outcome.

I'm not even suggesting that if you don't enjoy this area, you need to master this area. No, you don't need to, but an understanding and knowing that this type of thinking is most important at ground level will help you to develop a reasonable level of skill with regards to this thinking preference, so that you can at least understand other peoples' perspectives and then critically assess your alternatives or ideas.

We all need to develop our thinking preferences to a reasonable extent to become situationally holistic thinkers, as we discussed earlier.

With that, let's explore how to organize your thoughts, as organized thinking requires organizing your thought process first.

Four-Step Process to Organize Your Thoughts

By following the four steps below, you can start organizing your thoughts; that, in turn, will equip you to take specific actions with more confidence and calm.

1. Document your thoughts.

The first step is to empty your mind by documenting your thoughts. It's also important because there are times when we have ideas or thoughts about a multitude of things. If you don't get those things out of your head and documented in some way, you risk forgetting them or becoming overwhelmed with the sheer volume of your thoughts. There are enough references on the internet that our mind runs around 60,000 thoughts during a day. Of course, you can't document such a big number. And also, you don't need to, because more than 95% of those thoughts continue to repeat in our heads. Documenting your thoughts frees up your mind, as well, you can see them externally and give them some logical and sequential structure.

Use any mode of capturing the thoughts that work best for you, such as a pen and paper, text message, voice message, phone app, etc.

2. Sort your thoughts.

Now you can see all your thoughts on paper or wherever is comfortable for you. The next step is to sort all your thoughts, tasks, concerns, ideas, questions, etc., into their respective categories. For example, while documenting your thoughts, if you have noted your kid's education, your spouse's travel plan, your parents' medical check-up, or your family holiday planning, now is the time to give a broad category to these many listed thoughts – you can name it the Family Well-Being category.

Similarly, you can put all your thoughts into a few different categories. This will immediately organize your thoughts because instead of fifty scattered items on paper, you will probably not see more than five to seven categories. You'd agree that managing a limited number of organized categories is less overwhelming and easy to prioritize as compared to a vast number of scattered items.

3. Reframe your thoughts.

In the first step, your main emphasis was on just noting different kinds of thoughts down on paper so that you can free up your mind and see your thoughts from a distance – an important step before you categorize. However, in step two, while categorizing the thoughts into different buckets, you might realize that some of your thoughts need to be reframed to serve you better.

Reframing refers to changing the way a thought, concept, or idea is considered. This can be helpful when you are problem-solving. Looking at an issue in an alternate way may provide a viable solution that otherwise appears like a cumbersome or difficult task. For example, let's assume that you wrote a thought about how to imbibe self-discipline in your child so that she could study on her own. With that thought, you'll look for effective ways or techniques to build discipline. You could reframe the thought in a different way and ask yourself why she is not self-disciplined in the first place. Then you might reframe your thought about how you can provide her with some motivation instead of forcing discipline on her. With that reframed thought, you will look for ways to understand what intrinsically motivates her and what could drive her to study on her own.

4. Prioritize your thoughts

Now with necessary groundwork already done, this is the time to prioritize actions split into various categories. You have to move from a to-do list of items to assigning the deadlines or due dates in a calendar.

Due dates and deadlines are priorities based on importance and urgency. Many times, due dates and deadlines determine our priorities. Other times, our troubles cause us to worry, and those thoughts become our priority. Taking action on those worrisome thoughts, however small it may be, can possibly reduce the stress, so you can purposefully re-prioritize the thought for another time.

Use Mind-Mapping to Organize Your Thinking

You might think that you don't need to draw maps to organize your thinking and that you can simply jot down some of your thoughts using bullet points. This might work for some people, but it's not a very effective technique to organize your life. It's just one of the many ways to organize your schedule, but it doesn't lay out your thoughts.

Why is this?

Your mind works way faster than you can even imagine because it's all about billions of neurons wiring and firing with each other every fraction of a second. The kind of connections that this builds between different pieces of information in your memory and experience is exceptionally quick and difficult to fathom in a linear way. Also, these neuron connections are not linear; they are just random and instantaneous, as you may already have noted earlier about how thinking works inside the brain.

For example, you might be thinking about a breakfast meeting with your manager from abroad. Because your manager is coming from abroad, a connecting thought might pop up in your mind about planning your family vacations. Because you are now thinking about your family, your thoughts could then wander to shopping for your kids. Now, because you are thinking about your children, thoughts might also arise about the scheduled meeting with their schoolteacher the following Saturday. This example illustrates how our thoughts, while connected, don't follow any structure. Wouldn't it be exciting to see how these connections look on paper and what inferences you can draw?

Mind mapping is the technique in which you can see the interactions and connections happening between different thoughts in your brain. It's nothing but a visual diagram. A mind map is hierarchical and illustrates the relationship between different pieces of information.

Without putting your thoughts on paper, you might be able to organize the tasks, but you won't be putting your life in order. Failing to write down your thoughts will cause you to lose a lot of information in the process. That's why mind mapping is the best way to organize your thoughts and make the most optimal use of your thoughts by giving them a logical structure.

I've used mind mapping all the time, including when I used it to outline my book structure to counter the overwhelming flow of multiple ideas floating around in my mind. You can use mind mapping for any real-life situations where you must consider multiple factors that are interconnected.

Mind mapping helps people not only to organize their daily or weekly tasks but to aid and follow the natural process of thought. Thoughts can be overwhelming during a busy and even an ordinary day, and mind mapping helps you place them in the right order.

Once you have a mind map in front of you, you can enjoy the advantage of having access to all information on a single piece of paper. You don't have to roam your mind to organize the thoughts. You just follow branches and add your thoughts as you go.

Here is how you can do mind mapping:

Mind mapping begins with a central idea and then branches out into interconnected ideas related to that topic; these ideas can be shown as words or images. If you want to analyze various facets of a problem, mind mapping helps you to examine all of them together in a holistic manner to analyze the bigger picture.

For example, let's say that you want to start a new business. It will be in the center of your page; from there, you will branch out into connected ideas like your product, industry segment, targeted customer, competitors, financing needs, partners, time period, pricing, marketing, and other key challenges.

Mind mapping works on the principle that our thoughts are not ordered linearly. We looked at an example earlier, which demonstrated that, if you let one thought flow, it can lead you to endless random thoughts in any direction. Mind mapping is taking advantage of this nonlinear way our minds work.

Also, mind mapping makes you a balanced thinker. On one sheet of paper, you will start to see all your thoughts (i.e. your areas of concern) based on past experience, as well as how your imagination creates new solutions. Mind mapping can be equated to a marriage between logic and imagination. Our left brain creates logical, rational thought processes based on the crystallized intelligence we have gained over the years. On the other hand, our right brain uses imagery and colors and is creative and imagination-oriented. When you start building a mind map, you are employing whole-brain thinking by capturing your logic as well as imagination on a piece of paper.

You can create mind maps of all sorts. They could be about a career move, your next vacation, making choices amongst two different items, or planning for a perfect dinner party with friends.

How do you do it?

All you need to start is a topic, some colored pens, and a sheet of paper; follow these rules.

- Begin with a symbol or picture representing your topic in the center
- Write down key words or draw images on curved branches radiating from the center.
- Write one key word per line.
- Free associate and add smaller branches with images or words related to your key words.
- Use colors, pictures, dimensions and codes for greater association and emphasis.

By preparing a mind map, you'll be inserting your logic, calculations, and creative ideas about the situation, and thus, you will be using your left and right hemisphere; through this method of full brain thinking, you will find better solutions to your problems.

After you have created a mind map on paper in front of you or by using an app, you can easily make a step-by-step chart of activities that you can do in a sequential manner. This will allow you to see all the steps of any process and the nitty-gritty of any situation in a much more elaborate way.

Break it Down into Chunks of Fives and Tens

Did you ever think why social security numbers are given in chunks of three, two, and four (999-99-9999) instead of as one unbroken number (999999999)? Why do phone numbers have hyphens in them?

It's much easier to remember information when it's grouped into smaller chunks. I personally find that my brain prefers to remember things in groups of threes and fours, but maybe a group of four or eight would be your magic number.

Large blocks of information can be broken down into smaller chunks that are easier to remember. This process is called chunking and helps to speed up your mental processes because it organizes your stored memories into logical patterns. **You can use the same process to break complex ideas down into more logical pieces.**

For example, let's say that you are given the assignment of preparing a detailed safety program for a manufacturing plant. Instead of starting broadly at the plant level, you'll first divide it into separate departments or units. The next step will be to break it down further into different types of activities carried out within that department and the safety risk associated with each activity. Probably, the next step will be to break it down further into a smaller group of people who handle such activities and are responsible for safely carrying them out.

By devising a safety program for each unit by breaking the plan into smaller, more manageable chunks, what did you achieve?

First, it is not as overwhelming as preparing the safety plan for the entire plant in one go. Second, you can get started easily, as your unit of operation is very small. Third, once you prepare the initial safety plan for one unit, you'll get a base document, and from there, you'll approach the different units and make the necessary modifications as required for each specific unit. Once you have prepared plans for all units, you can organize the different pieces of information and then present a detailed factory level safety plan that will holistically cover the safety aspects of each unit, and you can make individual plans as annexes to that plan.

Above was just an example of the importance of breaking down the information into manageable pieces so you can organize them better and get your work done with more confidence instead of becoming overwhelmed with the vastness of the size of the activities.

This chunking method can be used for a wide variety of tasks, from recalling lists of items to remembering basic concepts, important points, or topics that you want to cover in a presentation at work or when approaching your boss for a raise. In a studying environment, if you're trying to figure out how to commit a long batch of notes to memory, see if you can break down your detailed notes into chunks of five main concepts. This will help you mentally organize all the material and recall the important facts.

Compartmentalization of Tasks and Prioritization

As you learned at the start of the chapter, in order to organize your thinking, your mind needs to think about how you can categorize or compartmentalize the activities into different boxes.

You know that by compartmentalizing the activities into different categories, you immediately reduce the vast number of items into smaller, more manageable chunks that are easier to prioritize.

Now let's look at one of the most effective ways to categorize the activities from the perspective of assigning deadlines or due dates so that you can really get going on those things.

You should prioritize your thoughts and the resulting action or actions. Understand what can wait and what needs to be addressed right now. Take everything but what you're working on and put it in a little box so that your mind remains as focused and productive as possible.

The Eisenhower Matrix is a great way to prioritize tasks into what needs to be done immediately, planned, delegated, or eliminated.

What is the **Eisenhower Matrix?**

Prior to becoming President of the U.S., Dwight Eisenhower served at senior positions in the army, including during World War II. During his time in the army, Eisenhower was faced with many tough decisions concerning the tasks he had to focus on every day. This led him to invent a principle that helps us prioritize our tasks by urgency and importance, which is famously known as the Eisenhower Matrix.

The Eisenhower Matrix results in four quadrants with various strategies as depicted and explained in the image below:

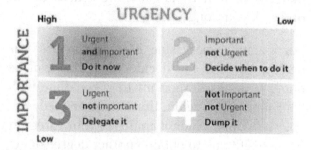

Quadrant 1: Do It Now

Quadrant 1 contains tasks that are both urgent and important. These are "do first" tasks because they are critical for your life or career in some way and need to be finished right away. You want to get these tasks done as soon as possible. These are the tasks that need to be done in order to avoid negative consequences. It is important to be able to manage the tasks that are in quadrant 1.

An example of a quadrant 1 task in your career may be answering a time-sensitive email from a client. This matrix can also be used in your personal life. An example of a quadrant 1 task in your personal life may be a crying baby, a medical emergency, or something burning in the oven.

Quadrant 2: Decide When

The tasks in quadrant 2 are important but not urgent. This is where you want to invest the majority of your time. Quadrant 2 tasks are in line with your long-term goals.

For example, exercising is important to your health, but you can decide when that can be done. It is also important to spend time with your family, but again, that can be aligned with your schedule. When it comes to your career, it may benefit you to obtain another degree or get a certificate of some sort. These things are important to your career, but they do not need to be done immediately.

It is important to remember here that just because these tasks are not urgent does not mean that they are not important. People often associate urgent matters with being important, which is not always true. Because your long-term goals generally stay constant, anything that will be beneficial to you in the long term will fall into the second quadrant.

Quadrant 3: Delegate It

The activities in this quadrant are urgent and, therefore, they may appear to be important. But if you pay attention to these activities and assess them from the perspective of your long-term goals, you will realize that someone else can do them instead of you. It will safeguard you from the anxiety and stress, relieve your workload, and free up additional units of time that you can devote to your quadrant 1 or quadrant 2 activities.

If you are in the middle of working on a project and the phone rings, it is not important for you to answer it. So, you can delegate this task to someone else. It may seem urgent at the time when it is happening, but these little things can be handled by other people.

Quadrant 4: Delete It

If something is neither important nor urgent, it falls into quadrant 4, and you want to avoid doing it. These tasks are simply a waste of your time, and they should be eliminated. If you are able to identify and eliminate all of your quadrant 4 tasks, you will free up some much-needed time to invest in your quadrant 2 tasks.

Some examples of quadrant 4 tasks are playing video games, binge-watching Netflix shows for hours merely for your entertainment, or just mindless web browsing.

I don't mean that entertainment shouldn't be part of your life at all. At times, you should take a break to wind down and rejuvenate yourself to better prepare for your next burst of productivity. But the problem happens when you spend too much time on quadrant 4 activities at the cost of your most important activities in quadrant 2.

Therefore, the challenge here is to spend most of your time in quadrant 2, and just enough time in quadrant 4 to get by.

Overall, the Eisenhower Matrix helps you to organize your thinking, as you have to compartmentalize tasks in such a way that you can devote your time, attention and efforts to activities that matter the most for you.

Declutter Your Space

Just have a quick look at your workstation. Is it clumsy and scattered, or is it organized? If the surrounding environment around you is scattered, that will affect your mind's ability to concentrate, as the scattered things will divert your attention from the work you are doing. It's difficult to organize your thoughts inside your mind if your outside environment is filthy and scattered.

In a study[4] conducted by Boyoun (Grace) Chae and Rui (Juliet) Zhu, 100 undergraduates were exposed to one of two environments. The first was a cluttered office with cups and boxes strewn around. The other was a neat and tidy desk. After exposure, the students were asked to do a task that was described to them as "challenging" — but the task was unsolvable. The results showed that the students exposed to the neat office stuck with the problem for an average of 18 minutes, while the ones who saw the messy desk could only focus for about 11 minutes on average.

---

[4] https://hbr.org/2015/01/why-a-messy-workspace-undermines-your-persistence

Also, being in a cluttered environment can make your brain feel claustrophobic. Set yourself up for logical, organized thinking by cleaning up and clearing out the space around you.

You can even turn it into a fun event by having a friend or family member help you decide what to keep and where to put things.

Use Online Tools to Organize Your Thinking

While the internet might be solely a source of distraction, such as social media sites or online news platforms, if wisely used, it's a treasure trove of resourceful information. It is not only a source of information; nowadays, there are so many websites, software, and mobile applications that can help you do many things with speed, precision and accuracy.

If you want to organize your thoughts and ideas in the form of mind maps, bullets, to-do-lists, calendars, or in any other manner, or if you want to organize your work in a systematic manner that manages your project, clients or customers seamlessly, you can find tools or applications for anything. I came across this useful article that provides 100 powerful tools to organize your thoughts and ideas[5]; you may find useful.

---

[5] https://www.online-college-blog.com/tips-and-

Chapter 5: Key Takeaways

An organized mode of thinking **enables you to make plans, create structures, and set up clear processes** for doing all the smaller steps necessary to carry out the desired action.

You can use the **4-step process to organize your thoughts.** Below are the four steps:

1. Document your thoughts.
2. Sort your thoughts.
3. Reframe your thoughts.
4. Prioritize your thoughts.

Following **mind-mapping techniques** helps you organize your thinking and enables you to holistically see the bigger picture. You can do mind mapping using simply a pen and paper, or you can use web applications or software to organize the scattered information in your brain, free your brain from clutter, and to perform a better analysis of the information that you have.

Both the compartmentalization and the prioritization of your thoughts are necessary for organized thinking. You can't organize any process or system unless you put them into different categories and assign timelines or deadlines to them. **The Eisenhower Matrix** is a great way to prioritize tasks into what needs to be done immediately, planned, delegated, or eliminated.

You need to **break the bigger information into small chunks**, as they are easier to memorize and handle. You can start more quickly with smaller chunks of activities, and it gives you a good starting point to base your future analysis on.

The way that you organize your workplace or desk directly affects your thinking approach. If your desk is cluttered, you will find it difficult to organize your thinking. A study proved that people who had organized desks were better able to focus more on their work and got better results.

In the age of technology, you can effectively **use various online tools and applications** to organize your thinking and ideas.

Chapter 6: Acquire Interpersonal Intelligence to Get Along With People

****

"We shall not perish as a people even if we get our money supply wrong — but if we get our human relationships wrong, we shall destroy ourselves."

~ Right Reverend Robert Runcie, Archbishop of Canterbury

Okay, we covered the logical/sequential left-brain thinking in the previous two chapters by learning the ways to improve your logical/rational thinking abilities as well as your sequential or organized thinking abilities.

Now let's shift the gears and come towards the right side of your brain. The right side is emotional, imaginative, and creative. As you learned in the previous chapter, this thinking preference is more inclined towards people. This is the segment of the brain that talks about teamwork and considers people to be the most important element in any decision-making process.

This aspect of thinking works on the principle that if you have a better connection with any individual, you have to communicate less and get the maximum impact. However, if you don't connect with someone at a deeper level, there will always be a communication gap; you won't be able to seek the full engagement of the person concerned. The precise equation can be framed as below:

A higher level of connection >> Lower need to communicate>> Better results

A lower level of connection >> Higher need to communicate >> Sub-optimal results

People who are not able to understand and empathize with others find it difficult to complete work requested from others and are not able to understand what others expect of them, so there will always be friction between them and other individuals.

Unless you are already more inclined toward this thinking preference, the techniques suggested in this chapter will help you be more empathetic towards others, solve the 'real' problems involving people much faster, and you will increase your chances of being liked by others in the process.

This section will help you improve your emotional brain by taking your interpersonal skills to the next level; these are the skills that we use when communicating and collaborating with others. You will learn effective ways to develop your interpersonal intelligence and skills.

Let's get started.

Never Automatically Attribute Malice to Others' Behavior

Do you sometimes feel that the whole world is against you? If something awful happens to you, you get a feeling that the world is not being fair to you, or there is some conspiracy going against you.

For example, if your manager is not able to give you time for discussion, you start thinking he doesn't like you, so you get scared that you won't receive a good appraisal this year. Or if you don't get a message from your friend for two days in a row, you imagine that he or she is not interested in you anymore. If the internet is not working in the cafe, you tend to think that the staff cheated you by hanging a board outside saying "free internet" merely to bring you into their shop.

Maybe you don't think that way, but you may have realized that many others do.

But here is the thing. Most of the time, these assumptions are just false stories created by our own minds. It might be that your boss was very busy working on some high-priority assignment and was worried about his or her career, so he couldn't attend the meeting with you. Maybe your friend was travelling on an important trip, and due to poor and infrequent network availability, he or she couldn't message you. Or there might have been some technical error in the servers of the internet service provider that cut off the internet availability at the cafe.

There could be many genuine reasons behind things happening around you, but it is the human tendency to assign malice to any motive, rather than to assume simple neglect or an innocent mistake. This happens because our minds have a natural tendency to automatically think negatively. Psychologists call this **"negativity bias."** This negativity bias was the reason humans could survive in the early days when they were living in forests or in dark caves and hunting animals for food. Because they were living in the forest, humans were consistently in the danger of being hunted and eaten by other wild animals. Any movement or sound in the jungle could be a threat to humans. In order to keep alert to all the dangers, our brain has an almond-sized organ called the amygdala. Also known as the fear center of our brain, it is responsible for giving directions to our body to either fight, flight, or freeze. Therefore, our first reaction to any situation is that there must be danger out there.

Fortunately, if you are reading this book on your electronic device, it means that you are not staying in any dangerous forest. It proves that you have access to the internet, a credit card, a smartphone, and are, therefore, living in a much safer environment. Most of the population is not subject to those dangers today because of technological developments. But the unfortunate part is that our brain's amygdala still perceives any kind of fear as a life or death situation, which is not the reality anymore. Instead of telling our mind that there is a genuine reason behind what happened, we get carried away by the negativity and start thinking adversely about any situation.

How can you overcome this malice-assigning tendency?

You can overcome this by using Hanlon's Razor Theory, which is a very effective mental model that states: *"Never attribute to malice that which can be adequately explained by neglect."*

The phrase "Hanlon's razor" was coined after Robert J. Hanlon, but it has been voiced by many people throughout history.

Napoleon Bonaparte also famously declared: "Never ascribe to malice that which is adequately explained by incompetence."

Goethe wrote similarly in *The Sorrows of Young Werther* in 1774: *"Misunderstandings and neglect create more confusion in this world than trickery and malice. At any rate, the last two are certainly much less frequent."*

Hanlon's razor can help you in situations when you deal with people, institutions, or entities you don't like. In such situations, your natural tendency is to assume those people have bad intentions toward you. Even their neutral behavior or actions might seem rude or aggressive to you. When such people make a mistake, you'd never react with empathy or understanding toward that person.

Here, it's important to apply Hanlon's razor, because this theory will help you to put your preconceived notions aside and assess the other side's behavior with a clear and neutral mindset. Applying Hanlon's razor in our day-to-day lives allows us to develop better relationships and become less judgmental and more rational. **Hanlon's razor allows us to give people the benefit of the doubt and have more empathy.**

Hanlon's razor can be utilized in most situations as a rule of thumb; however, as with everything else, there are exceptions to this rule. If you have empirical evidence or information that supports the malice on the part of the other side, then you need to be careful when dealing with such a person. For example, if someone is coming toward you with a knife in his hands, this rule doesn't apply. Here, you need to listen to your amygdala's instructions and be prepared to handle the situation.

Therefore, in order to boost your interpersonal thinking skills, in most cases, you need to remove the element of assumption of malice in other people's behavior. Hanlon's Razor theory can save you lots of time, effort, and energy that goes into countering the 'assumed' malice, which can be easily justified by ignorance or stupidity even.

Moreover, when you deal with people without any kind of false assumptions and are genuine, you develop connections at a much deeper level.

Develop Active Listening Skills

Active listening is the process by which an individual secures information from another individual or group. The "active" element involves taking steps to draw out details that might not otherwise be shared. Active listeners avoid interrupting at all costs, summarize and repeat back what they have heard, and observe body language to give them an extra level of understanding.

Active listening is a helpful skill for any individual to develop. It helps you to truly understand what people are saying in conversations and meetings (and not just what you *want* to hear or *think* that you hear). During interviews, it can help you to build rapport with your interviewer.

Active listening redirects your focus from what is going on inside of your head to the needs of your prospective employer or interviewer. That can help reduce your nervousness during an interview.

Here is how you can develop active listening skills:

- **Building trust:** You should ask the other person how you can help him or her. Genuinely appreciating some of the good aspects of the other person goes a long way to build trust and rapport.

- **Demonstrating concerns:** If the other person is going through some tough times, you should offer a helping hand and demonstrate genuine concern.

- **Paraphrasing:** Actively listening will help you understand the subject better and, therefore, paraphrasing what the other person has said is a good way to show that you are attentive to him or her.

- **Non-verbal cues:** Nodding the head or giving a thumbs up if you agree with the concept shows that you are actively listening to the other person.

- **Brief verbal affirmations** like "I see," "I know," "Sure," "Thank you," or "I understand" give the other person a clear message that he is being attended.

- **Asking open-ended questions:** Open-ended questions don't have a clear structure and, therefore, prompt the other person to give his/her wider perspective, and there is enough material to actively listen to.

- **Asking specific questions** to seek clarification is important to get a clearer understanding.

- **Don't just wait to disclose your opinion**: Don't just wait until the other person finishes to disclose your opinion. This adversely impacts your listening skills because instead of weighing the other person's thoughts, you are just thinking about what you will say when your turn comes.

- **Disclosing similar experiences** to show understanding. This helps to build in a sense of commonality with the other person.

While the above tactics will help you to build effective communication skills, you need to be careful enough to avoid a few common communication blockers. **Here are the most common roadblocks to communication; they can stop communication dead in its tracks**:

- **"Why" questions**: They tend to make people defensive.

- **Quick reassurance**: For example, saying things like, "Don't worry about that."

- **Advising**: "I think the best thing for you is to move into assisted living."

- **Digging for information:** Forcing someone to talk about something that they would rather not talk about.

- **Patronizing**: "You poor thing; I know just how you feel."

- **Preaching**: "You should. . ." or, "You shouldn't. . ."

- **Interrupting**: Shows you aren't interested in what someone is saying.

If you follow the above techniques and avoid hitting the roadblocks, you will strongly develop your active listening skills, and that, in turn, will help you boost your interpersonal thinking. This will enable you to take the interpersonal aspects into account before making big decisions.

Widen Your Circle of People to be More Empathic

Empathy, especially for strangers, starts with exposure to people who are different than us. Research has found that contact with people of different races increases our empathy toward them at a neurological level. So if you want to increase your empathy, widen your circle.

In one fascinating study[6] at the University of Queensland, Australia, psychologist Yuan Cao and her colleagues found that exposure to groups that are racially different than us can increase the empathy we feel toward those groups when we see them in pain.

In the study, 23 Chinese immigrants were shown videos of actors – some Chinese and some Caucasian (of European origin) – receiving a painful touch of a syringe needle to the face. They examined the participant's brains while they watched the videos using fMRI technology – and what they found is truly astounding.

The Chinese immigrants reacted more strongly to the videos of the Chinese actors in pain than the Caucasians. But that's not all. The Chinese immigrants who reported more contact with Caucasians in their lives showed greater empathetic responses to the Caucasian actors, showing that this tendency to show more empathy toward our "in-group" is a malleable characteristic. The sample is small, but it's a fascinating study that needs to be replicated.

---

[6] https://espace.library.uq.edu.au/view/UQ:355349

These findings indicate that one answer to the question of how to increase your empathy, in the broadest sense of the term, is simply to interact with more people, especially people from a different "group" than yours.

Reading Literary Fiction Enhances Your Empathy

Reading literary fiction, specifically, has been shown to improve empathy. These findings come from a fascinating series of studies[7] led by Emanuele Castano, a social psychologist at The New School in New York City. In the studies, participants were split up into different reading groups based on genre: popular fiction, literary fiction, nonfiction, or nothing – and then given a test to measure their ability to infer and understand other people's emotions.

The findings were remarkable. When the participants read nothing, non-fiction, or popular fiction, their results were unimpressive. But reading literary fiction led to big increases in the reader's ability to empathize.

How could this be?

---

[7]
http://www.newschool.edu/pressroom/pressreleases/2013/CastanoKidd.htm

Literary fiction books tend to look into the psychological complexities of characters. These interesting, complex characters drive the story, and we, as readers, are emotionally involved in their desires and motivations. The inner lives of the characters are not easily discerned but rather warrant deeper exploration, which is often revealed in layers throughout the book.

It turns out that when it comes to improving empathy, it's perfectly fine to practice on fictional characters.

Imagine the possibilities here. You may not be able to hang out with a family of undocumented immigrants, or someone living in war-torn Mosul, Iraq, but that doesn't mean you can't actively increase your empathy for them. Through literary fiction, we can practice empathy globally – helpful, and even essential, in a complex, globalized world.

Make Curiosity a Habit to Improve Your Empathy

The **switch from judgment to curiosity** is a crucial step for anyone who wants to increase their empathy for others. Whether it's with friends, coworkers, or complete strangers, we too often judge others based on our own assumptions.

But we can teach ourselves to make a habit out of curiosity, switching from thinking that we know what's going on to genuinely wondering what's going on. The mental shift is subtle, but it can change our perspective in a big way. Consider the following situation.

The story (what you see): You are at the grocery store, and in between you and your favorite yogurt is a toddler having a complete meltdown. The mother seems to have lost control and is standing there, not really doing or saying much at all.

Your judgment (what you label the story): She is a terrible mother. I mean, look at her kid! He's acting like a hurricane, and she's not doing anything! Some people shouldn't have kids until they are ready.

Switch to curiosity (don't label; understand the real facts): That mom doesn't seem to be doing anything while her kid has a meltdown. I wonder what is going on with her. Maybe she is overwhelmed, sleep-deprived, tired of the terrible twos, or unsure of what to do? Maybe she could use a hug and some reassurance that everything will be okay?

If you introduce a dose of curiosity into your thinking instead of judging every situation,

143

you'll get to know the other person's perspective. Being judgmental immediately surrounds you with false self-created boundaries; you don't let other people inside. But when you switch from judgmental behavior to being curious about what's really happening, you open up. Now you don't have any judgment, so you have the genuine intention of knowing exactly what's happening behind the scenes. When you are sincere and curious to know about other people, they can see through it, they can feel the warmth and authentic concern you have towards them, and then they reciprocate in sharing their truth.

Switching from judgment to curiosity builds your empathy towards others and broadens your perspective about the interpersonal aspects of human behavior.

Challenge yourself to have a deeper conversation with a colleague.

Understanding a person's point of view or personal challenges requires a conversation that moves past the weather. This doesn't mean that you should ask your colleague about highly personal matters. Start by sharing a little more of your own experiences and perspectives, and see if your colleague follows suit.

It's an excellent way to jump in the waters of improving empathy. While you speak to this person, think about using their name, smiling, encouraging them, and listening without interrupting. This singular conversation won't just be practice; it will lay the foundation for a better working relationship with your colleague. You also might enjoy it yourself!

Here are a few quick activities that can help you engage in, learn, and better access interpersonal thinking:

- Come up with a 'fun' event idea for the people at your workplace, and make it happen.
- Look for ways to make your workspace more fun, comfortable and entertaining.
- Offer to mentor or coach a coworker or employee.
- Make a decision totally based on the team consensus.
- Use some app or tool to remind yourself to connect with other people on a regular basis for 15 minutes a day.

Chapter 6: Key Takeaways

The act of thinking is not merely a rational or logical approach; you need to also nurture the emotional and instinctual side of your brain.

An interpersonal thinking approach **empowers you to connect with people more effectively** and get results faster. The formula for getting results is as follows:

The higher the level of connection, the less that communication is needed, and the better the results. **The lower the level of connection**, the more communication is needed, and the results are less than optimal.

The following techniques can be used for developing interpersonal thinking:

Follow **Hanlon's Razor**; don't see malice or bad intention in a situation that can be justified by some genuine lapses.

Active Listening: You can build trust with the other people by following active listening skills to demonstrate concern using non-verbal cues, brief verbal affirmations, or disclosing similar experiences.

Make curiosity as a habit to develop empathy. Withhold your judgment of any individual, and display curiosity about their behavior.

Widen your circle by meeting new people and more people so that you can understand their concerns. You should especially meet people from other cultural or socio-economic groups than yours.

Reading literary fiction heightens your level of empathy for others, and thus, it develops your interpersonal thinking abilities.

Challenge yourself to have deeper conversations with your colleagues. When you deeply engage in conversation with someone, you understand the underlying emotions and feelings of the other person. You come to know and understand the key drivers or motivators that affect the person's behavior.

Chapter 7: Unleash Creative Thinking to Explore Endless Possibilities

****

"Creativity is intelligence having fun."

~ Albert Einstein

Without creativity, it's not possible to come up with many good alternatives to solve your problems. Your thinking becomes stagnant if you don't use your mind's creative abilities.

Most people, if asked about their views about creativity, would think of some type of artist with long hair, so deeply immersed in their art that they wouldn't care about how they look to the outside world – almost an odd one out kind of person.

But that's not the right way to look at creativity. In fact, creativity is not some unique domain reserved specifically for artists, writers or musicians, or any other so-called 'creatives'. Rather, it's one of the most important skills in the modern business world.

As per one recent IBM study[8] titled *Capitalizing on Complexity*, which was based on face-to-face interaction with the top 1500 chief executive officers worldwide, one of the top three key traits that leaders are looking for in their talent is creative thinking.

If you're reading this book and you lack creative-thinking abilities, you won't be able to tap into the full potential of your brain. This chapter will change how you perceive creativity while stripping creativity itself of its mystique. Trust me; if you can generate ideas that deliver results, they will have the potential to shift the trajectory of your personal, work, and all the other aspects of your life.

Let's first briefly examine what creativity is.

Professor Margaret Boden, from the University of Sussex, has been researching the science of creativity for more than 30 years, and she has explained the concept of creativity in the detailed manner below:

*"Creativity is a **fundamental feature of human intelligence** in general. It is grounded in everyday capacities, such as the association of ideas, reminding, perception, analogical thinking, searching a structured problem-space, and reflecting self-criticism. It involves not only a cognitive dimension (the*

---

[8] https://www.ibm.com/downloads/cas/1VZV5X8J

generation of new ideas) but also motivation and emotion, and is closely linked to cultural context and personality factors."

This section is all about learning the most effective ways to improve an individual's creative thinking abilities. But the very first step to boost your creative thinking abilities is to change your belief about your capacity for creativity. If, somehow, you think, like most people, that creativity is a domain reserved for only a few people, then you need to open up your mind and be willing to explore the possibilities.

Your Beliefs Can Make You More Creative

Merely believing that you're a creative person starts to improve your creativity. There was a study conducted in a major publishing company to find out why some people were creative and others were not. The results of the study surprised everyone because, all other things being equal, there was only one factor that determined whether someone would be creative or not.

Here is what the results showed: The members of the group who believed that they were creative were creative, and the members of the other group of people who believed otherwise were not creative.

This is a surprisingly simple but profound concept.

The study didn't stop there. As a next step, the company organized some training for the individuals who did not believe that they were creative to teach them some effective strategies to build their belief system. The results of the training were astonishing. All of them started giving way more creative solutions and innovative ideas than the earlier set of creative people, who already believed they were creative.

That's the power of positive belief in anything you want in life. In my other book, *Think Out of the Box*, I've mentioned many effective strategies to build a powerful belief system to become a more creative thinker.

Strong belief is the first requirement for building creative thinking skills. It's within your control to replace your beliefs by reinforcing a new belief system through some proven ways, but you will need the step-by-step method for creative thinking that we have provided below.

6 Steps to Creative Thinking

In 1926, the English social psychologist and co-founder of the London School of Economics, Graham Wallas, shared his model of creativity, a way of understanding how original ideas form in the mind and are carried into the world. He penned a book titled *The Art of Thought*, wherein he shared four stages of creativity based both on his own empirical observations and on the accounts of famous inventors and polymaths. These four stages are **preparation, incubation, insights,** and **verification.**

However, Ned Herrmann, the originator of HBDI system, added two more stages to it: one at the start, namely 'interest', and other one at the end of the above 4-stage process, which he called 'application'. He stated that before the creativity process starts (with preparation), the individual must have an interest in the subject matter. The interest comes from an individual's intrinsic motivation, meaning that his/her satisfaction comes from the work itself. He mentioned further that a person would continue to strive in difficult times only if he/she is intrinsically driven (motivated for inner reasons) to do so, because the reward would not be coming from some distant place; rather, it would be instant. In other words, when a person is sincerely interested in some subject, he gets the instant reward of satisfaction from the work itself.

Regarding the other element, Herrmann explained that after verification, i.e. the last stage of Wallas' 4-step model, there has to be an application of the creative process to the real world. Verification is the experiment done in the constraints of test environment, which is controlled, but the application of the idea needs to pass through the uncontrollable and unknown parameters that come only when you apply it in the real world. Only then will your ideas be proven or disproven.

Accordingly, the six stage creativity process is as shown below.

Stage 1: **Interest**

Stage 2: **Preparation**

Stage 3: **Incubation**

Stage 4: **Illumination**

Stage 5: **Verification**

Stage 6: **Application**

Let's have a look at each of these stages in detail:

Interest is very critical to engaging in the creative process. To reiterate, without it, you can't really get started. You can have interest for a wide variety of reasons. For example, it may start with an urge to solve an issue, curiosity, the desire to deal with a human need, or an intriguing technical challenge. Interest in the project is the necessary fuel for the process to get initiated.

The second stage of the process is preparation. This step requires gathering information, analyzing the facts, and the chronological sequencing of those facts into accurate statements of the problem.

Let's understand this by way of an example. Let's assume that you work for a company that plans to come out with a huge amusement park in the town to cater to the needs of children and adults for their weekly entertainment or as an adventure destination for visitors. Your role is to come up with unique and attractive games or adventure activities that attract people from various backgrounds and demographic groups. Setting up an amusement and adventure park is a huge project, and coming up with a unique approach to make your amusement park look special and attractive to potential customers requires careful thinking and planning. Preparation is essential in order to generate new ideas. You'll need to do lots of research and find as much relevant information as possible.

Here is what you'll do.

You'll use free as well as paid tools to do your research. You'll do internet research about all the adventure parks in the vicinity or in distant places. You'll also want to visit a few such places and have the real experience of going on various rides and participating in many games to get an idea of what they are all about. Maybe you'll make some connections or talk to friends or to distant family about different amusement parks that they have visited and ask what they liked about them. If situations allow, you'd want to travel to far-off places, or even foreign countries, to get some new ideas about how things change with culture and geographies and to take the interpersonal human element into account.

If the entertainment industry is your key interest, then your preparation will include some research about the human psychology behind entertainment and what triggers people emotionally to spend money in such places.

In the preparation stage, the exact problem to be solved needs to be defined and stated. Let's say that the problem is, "How can I create a highly entertaining, thrilling, and joyful experience for a group of people, whether it is a family, friends, or teenagers? How can I be sure that they will recommend this experience to others?" An analysis of the target audience needs to be made; as well, you would need to know how to install the latest technology support, as well as what technically sound and safe equipment can be installed at your amusement park. The preparation stage requires using both quadrant A and B thinking approaches.

The next phase of the process involves incubation. This is where the brain, which now has a problem to work on and is strongly motivated by personal interest, processes that problem with both the conscious and unconscious mind, which allows the brain's natural problem-solving processes to be engaged.

This incubation stage of the creative process clearly draws more on the C and D types of mental activities, making use of intuitive and conceptual understanding to bring potential solutions to a conscious level. It often works best when we are totally disengaged from the task at hand and are relaxed or tinkering with something else.

After you've defined the problem and collected the facts, immerse yourself in all of this information. Your brain will make connections as you visit a few amusement parks, soak up the experiences of different fun activities, and see the thrilled and joyful expressions on the faces of other people. You are not consciously looking for solutions in this stage; you are simply going about your day in a relaxed manner. Sometimes incubation can take a few hours, and other times, you will continue to incubate as the preparation process continues. This creative problem-solving process does not happen in a neat, chronological manner. An iteration between stages is often necessary before ideas begin to emerge.

The next stage is called illumination, which is frequently referred to as the 'aha' or 'eureka moment' in the creative process. This is where ideas suddenly pop into our minds as potential solutions. The illumination stage integrates all the aspects of the creative process that took place in the interest, preparation, and incubation stages. And through integration, synthesis, and synergy, ideas present themselves in response to everything that has happened along the way.

The Greek mathematician, Archimedes, is one of the most well-known examples when it comes to the concept of illumination. Here is his quick story. He was asked by a king, who was suspecting that a golden crown contained more silver than gold, to devise a method whereby one could know the purity of a metal.

Archimedes spent days and nights on this problem, but he couldn't find the answer. Then he put the problem aside and took a hot bath in the tub. As he was relaxing in the hot bath, he realized that the water overflowed when he put his body in the water, and this realization paved the way for a unique solution to his problem. He concluded that a pure gold crown would displace a different amount of water than the one made by an alloy. The history records that he was so excited to find this answer that he ran naked out of his bed in the streets shouting "Eureka"! (I've found it!).

Let's look at our example of creating a unique idea about setting up an amusement park. Now you have dedicated enough hours to researching different project parameters, visited numerous locations, and tried different rides to immerse yourself in the real amusement park experience. But you are worried that you still have not come up with a unique, groundbreaking idea. There are two networks that will enable you to do this. One is an active network; that's what you have used so far in your preparation and incubation stages. The other network is a 'default mode network' (DMN) where you let your mind wander wherever it desires and let it build some unique connections with the information it already has. Now is the time to sit back and relax a bit. Now, you need to get totally disengaged from your work and let your mind wander. This default mode network is responsible for your imagination and idea insights. That's why most CEOs or top executives are found saying that their unique ideas generally pop up when they are in the shower or when they are enjoying vacations. Your subconscious mind needs some space to formulate unique combinations and create new ideas through fusion.

Don't force your mind to generate ideas mechanically. Instead, if you let serendipity take over, there is a strong probability that you'll get your insights sooner rather than later. Ideas don't have a timetable; they can come in minutes, or they may even take days or weeks. However, if you are open to relinquishing control over your thoughts, this will speed up the process.

> *"Without this playing with fantasy, no creative work has ever yet come to birth. The debt we owe to the play of imagination is incalculable."*
>
> —*Carl Jung*

The next stage that is needed is verification, which requires a hard-nosed, objective review of the potential solutions in relation to the facts of the original problem. Does this new idea have any relationship to the original problem that you were attempting to solve? Verification is necessary, since the idea-generating activity that results from the illumination process can come up with a multitude of potential ideas, some of which have no relationship at all to the problem at hand. But who knows? They may, in fact, be solutions to problems that have not yet been defined.

The prerequisite for finding good ideas is to generate lots and lots of ideas, so that you can mine out the best one among them.

The way to get good ideas is to get lots of ideas and throw the bad ones away.

—Linus Pauling

Therefore, a critical assessment of the appropriateness of the potential solution has to take place before that potential solution can be applied. Once again, you'll need to draw more on quadrant A and B thinking approaches that take particular advantage of the critical, diagnostic, and analytic capabilities of the A quadrant.

Now that you have some potential solutions, you need to critically assess their relationship to the problem. Is a particular solution feasible? Will it truly give a unique and thrilling experience to your target audience? You might think this solution will work for your needs, but you have to check it out.

After you have critically verified a solution, application is the next step in the process. This six-step process is actually a whole-brain thinking process in its entirety, but it starts with more of a B-quadrant-oriented focus on implementation, with some analysis from quadrant A, interaction with the customer in quadrant C, and taking into account the big picture and the whole application process in quadrant D. As you attempt your initial applications, you may need to revisit the verification process.

Does the potential solution fit the original problem, and is the application viable? Does the thing really work? Is there anything else that you need to do to make it work? And when you finally make the necessary adjustments, does the idea solve the original problem?

Let's understand this application aspect of the idea stages with an example. A developer at the adhesive company 3M was verifying an idea (creating a special adhesive) that emerged during the illumination stage; it didn't meet the verification process.

In trying to create an adhesive that was very thin but extremely strong, the developer created a glue that was easily applied; but it wasn't permanent enough to be what the company was looking for.

Later on, a 3M colleague, an inventor and scientist named Arthur Fry, had been in church for choir practice, grappling with a regularly occurring problem with his hymnbook: Fry would bookmark his hymnbook with pieces of paper, but by Sunday morning, they would have fallen out. Arthur had a moment of illumination. Here was the perfect application for this faulty adhesive: a nonpermanent way to stick memos to hymnals—or anything else! Yes – the birth of Post-it Notes.

Even though this particular adhesive didn't meet the requirements for the original application, another eureka moment pointed to a completely different application that could easily have been discarded. The next process step, application, brought the Post-it Notes product we know today to the world of additional uses.

This idea illustrates how an idea that failed to solve the original problem served as the best solution to another problem.

Each New Idea Extends From the Past and Moves into the Future

"Look back to see where ideas came from and then look ahead to discover where those ideas may lead. A new idea is a beginning, not an end. Ideas are rare— milk them. Following the consequences of small ideas can result in big payoffs."

~Edward D. Berger and Michael Starbird

Ideas don't exist or get created in a vacuum. Someone rightly said that creativity is all about the fusion of memory and imagination. Memory comes from your past experiences, and imagination is all about thinking about the future. When you allow the fusion of your past memories with new thoughts about the future, ideas start to germinate.

Each new idea extends into a line started from the past and passing through the present to travel into the future.

Do you know how calculus came into existence?

If you don't know, calculus is the mathematical study of continuous change, in the same way that geometry is the study of shape, and algebra is the study of generalizations of arithmetic operations.

Isaac Newton and Gottfried Leibniz seem to have invented calculus on their own at the end of the 17th century. But it was noted that early historians had already discovered the essential elements of calculus way before Newton and Leibniz came along. Newton himself said that, "If I have seen further than others, it is by standing on the shoulders of giants."

Calculus truly changed the world; but it didn't change the world on the day it was discovered. During the past three centuries, calculus has been applied to mechanics, to the motion of the planets, to electricity and magnetism, to fluid flow, to biology, to economics, as well as to countless other areas. Calculus is an example of how far an idea can be pushed. Leibniz published the first article on calculus in 1684: an essay that was a mere six pages long. But today's introductory calculus textbook contains over 1,300 pages. A calculus textbook introduces two fundamental ideas, and the remaining 1,294 pages consist of examples, variations, and applications—all arising from following the consequences of just two fundamental ideas.

Therefore, every subject is an ongoing journey of discovery and development. It's not a laundry list of disconnected ideas but different ideas that are cohesive and build upon one another. When we see and understand that these ideas are connected, they become more interesting, more memorable, and more meaningful.

Step into the Intersection — The Medici Effect

Frans Johansson, the author of *The Medici Effect*, explored another simple yet profound insight about innovation when he said, "**in the intersection of different fields, disciplines and cultures**, there's an abundance of extraordinary new ideas to be explored."

Putting together ideas from different areas — ideas that were always seen as completely apart — can easily generate an explosion of new ideas. And since the best way to have great ideas is to have lots of ideas, the best chances for innovation are at those intersections.

The book makes a case for learning broadly and the importance of keeping a curious attitude. This comes as an inspiring invitation to explore areas other than our own and as a reminder to always pursue our side interests. Johansson shares many interesting stories of cross-pollination between disciplines: ecologists helping logistics experts to plan truck routes more efficiently, or astronomers unintentionally unraveling old ecology mysteries; the intersections are literally everywhere.

Why do so many world-changing insights come from people with little or no related experience? Charles Darwin was a geologist when he proposed the theory of evolution. And it was an astronomer who finally explained what happened to the dinosaurs.

Frans Johansson's The Medici Effect shows how breakthrough ideas most often occur when we bring concepts from one field into a new, unfamiliar territory, and offers examples how we can turn the ideas we discover into path-breaking innovations.

Along similar lines, Justin Musk (Elon Musk's ex-wife), also puts it beautifully in the words below:

*"Choose one thing and become a master of it. Choose a second thing and become a master of that. **When you become a master of two worlds** (say, engineering and business), you can bring them together in a way that will a) introduce hot ideas to each other, **so they can have idea sex and make idea babies** that no one has seen before and b) create a competitive advantage because you can move between worlds, speak both languages, connect the tribes, and mash the elements to spark fresh creative insight until you wake up with the epiphany that changes your life."*

HOW TO LEVEL UP CREATIVE THINKING AND GENERATE IDEAS

Ask questions to generate ideas.

"The unexamined life is not worth living." — Socrates

Socrates is most famous for generating ideas by asking uncomfortable core questions.

Constantly formulating and asking questions is a mind-opening habit that will permit you to have a deeper engagement with the world and a broadening of your inner experience. Great innovators always ask a variety of questions every time they encounter some problem or challenge.

It's the quality of question that determines the quality of life. Questions cause you to stretch, grow, and think beyond what's real on the ground and activate your imagination.

Questions bring you out of the certainty of knowledge and lead you to an uncertain world you are not familiar with. Certainty narrows your worldview, and uncertainty broadens and deepens your understanding. When you know that you are certain, you don't explore much; but when you invite uncertainty in your life, you want to come out with better ideas.

Eugene Ionesco says, "It is not the answer that enlightens but the question."

Isaac Newton asked, "Why does an apple fall from a tree?" and "Why does the moon not fall into the Earth?"

Here is what Albert Einstein said about curiosity and the power of questions:

"Don't think about why you question; simply don't stop questioning. Don't worry about what you can't answer, and don't try to explain what you can't know. Curiosity is its own reason. Aren't you in awe when you contemplate the mysteries of eternity, of life, of the marvelous structure behind reality? And

this is the miracle of the human mind—to use its constructions, concepts, and formulas as tools to explain what man sees, feels, and touches. Try to comprehend a little more each day. Have holy curiosity."

Therefore, to generate a new set of ideas, ask a newer set of questions. To give you some specifics, ask questions for all types of interrogative prefixes like:

- Why
- What
- Who
- When
- How
- Where
- Whether
- If

Take a pen and paper and list your most important projects with regards to your personal life, work, relationship, family, adventure, and spirituality, and ask any questions that come up about why things are the way they are, what you can do to improve the situation, who can help you to generate more ideas, and where you can find such person.

Figure out how to carry out the great ideas that you get exposed to, and let the ideas keep popping up. Keep writing whatever comes to your mind. You'll either find the answers, trigger some more leading questions about further research, meet some people, or do some experiments. If you do this sincerely, you'll surely generate tons of ideas, and hopefully, some of them may serve as your breakthrough ideas that can transform the way that you work.

But the key is to keep asking yourself questions. Don't accept the status quo, and don't let life keep moving as it has been — in only one direction. You can generate unique, new ideas with the right set of questions.

Do SCAMPER — Get Loads of Ideas Instantly!

The SCAMPER method offers you a checklist for idea-spurring questions. It provides a structured way of assisting students to think out of the box. The SCAMPER method was proposed in 1953 by Alex Faickney Osborn, an advertising executive and author, and was further developed in 1971 by Bob Eberle in his book, *SCAMPER: Games for Imagination Development*.

The seven-letter acronym describes how you can generate multiple ideas by dividing your challenge or project into different stages and brainstorming ideas by asking the following questions about each stage.

- S = **Substitute** something
- C = **Combine** it with something else
- A = **Adapt** something to it
- M = **Modify** or Magnify it
- P = **Put it** to some different use
- E = **Eliminate** something
- R = **Reverse-engineer** it.

How to use the SCAMPER technique:

Step 1: **Isolate your challenge into different parts** or stages.

Step 2: After that, **apply each of the seven elements of the SCAMPER method to each of the stages** of your project to ask questions and generate ideas.

Actually, your mind has an unlimited potential that needs to be tapped by asking the right set of questions, and the SCAMPER method does the very same thing by asking a different set of questions in an intelligent manner. SCAMPER offers subtle cues or triggers that trigger your mind to come out with various alternatives.

How to implement SCAMPER in your personal or work life:

Just think about one of the meaningful projects that you want to succeed in by applying innovative and creative thinking. After you have finalized the project, divide the project into as many small steps as it makes sense to do in a way that each step can be ascertained separately.

Now, take any one stage of your important project and apply each of the SCAMPER questions to that step, and keep noting down different ideas on your note pad or laptop.

Apply SCAMPER to each of the steps, and keep jotting down all the ideas coming to you.

Once you are done, start looking at the ideas that you have generated. I'm sure that you will produce way more ideas than you would get by just thinking ordinarily.

Magic Wand Thinking Technique

What if you had a magic wand and you were able to solve this problem with no constraints as to what the solution might look like?

Most often we nip an idea in the bud even before it starts to blossom due to our assumptions or limiting beliefs about the likelihood of the fruition of that idea. When we start out on our journey to develop creative thinking skills, we may often experience roadblocks. They are from outside as well as from inside your mind; you can call them idea killers.

Now, instead of killing your ideas, you should kill these 'idea killers'. Let's look at a list of a few idea killers (you can expand it further depending upon your personal experience and life situations):

- Don't be ridiculous.
- We tried that before.
- We have never done it before.
- We don't have time.
- We are too small for this.
- We don't have necessary manpower or bandwidth to handle this.
- Let's get back to reality.
- You can't teach an old dog a new technique.
- That's not practical.
- It's not in our budget.

Another key problem is that we mistakenly think that we lack time, resources, energy, or the right kind of people to execute some of our ideas, so we rule out some ideas before even putting them at the paper.

Tony Robbins rightly said once that it's not lack of resources but a lack of resourcefulness that prevents you from making progress toward your dreams and goals.

Every day, you find bootstrapping startups initiated by twenty-year-olds who get funding to take their business to the next level. You see, they don't have the resources, but they have the resourceful mindset, and with that, they attract the funds, expertise, and support from angel investors.

If you can temporarily silence your inner critic, hold an imaginary magic wand in your hand that can do anything you desire, and then list the things that can be done, you'll be amazed by the volume of crazy ideas that will shower upon you. The key point is to write them all down first, before they fly away.

Ideas are like tiny butterflies, and they fly away if you let them pass by, thinking that you'll capture them later. A new idea can fly away in a matter of seconds if you don't capture it, and after some time passes, you won't even recall what it was. Therefore, the first step is to write down whatever comes to your mind while holding the magic wand and then later, use your logical and rational thinking approach to test them out. Of course, many of them will be bad, but when you put your magic wand down, a few ideas may still stand out if you just tweak them and look at them with an open perspective.

Set Up a Daily Idea Quota

James Altucher, in his book titled "Become an Idea Machine," recommends coming up with 10 new ideas every day. It doesn't matter if they are good or bad. The key is to exercise your "idea muscle" to keep it toned and in great shape.

Developing ideas is also like building muscles. If you want to build muscles, you work out with heavier weights and stretch your muscles. You need to do the same with your ideas as well. Stretch your imagination, and set a quota for yourself to come up with a specific number of ideas every day.

In the world of creativity, the greater the number of ideas, the better your choice will be. Quantity of ideas will lead to quality of ideas. Making a habit of generating a fixed quota of ideas per day works better as it will discipline your mind to actively generate ideas rather than waiting for them to occur to you.

You can start by generating five ideas every day for a week in relation to your challenges. It will be hard initially, but once you start putting them down on paper, they will start connecting and lead you to better ideas. Then, look at the stock of ideas you generated over the course of the week, and identify the winning ideas worth implementing for your important projects. You may find one or two ideas that you can start implementing related to your most important projects.

The TLC Technique

There is another technique to even make use of crazy ideas that don't seem to be feasible at a given point of time. Use the TLC technique, which is an acronym that stands for three inquisitive questions, namely (a) Tempting; (b) Lacking; and (c) Change

To turn crazy ideas into actionable solutions, you should ask three questions:

What's **tempting** about this idea?

What's **lacking** in this idea?

What could I **change** to make this idea work?

By following the TLC technique, you don't let your ideas go waste, as you can use the TLC questions to dig deeper into any idea to understand the pros and cons and then modify the idea to make it work for any specific problem or create something unique that doesn't exist already.

Idea Crowdsourcing: How to Generate Quick Ideas from a Group of People

What is 1 + 1? Of course, the mathematical answer is 2, but when it comes to the power of people, the answer become 11.

That's true for idea generation as well. When two or more people generate ideas simultaneously on a given problem, that can open up a realm of new possibilities. What if you know some technique where you can quickly generate ideas from a group of people? One such technique is known as the Crawford Slip Writing Method.

It is a simple, yet effective type of brainstorming technique that gives the opinions of all team members equal weight, regardless of how quiet they are. It is actually one of the original forms of brainwriting, which is an easy-to-use, effective group survey tool that rapidly and anonymously enables the collection of ideas from audiences of almost any size.

The Crawford Slip Writing is often the most efficient means of generating ideas and organizing them quickly into categories. This creativity technique is mainly used for:

1. Obtaining written information, ideas, and suggestions from individuals in a group setting;

2. Analyzing and synthesizing the data gathered; and

3. Reporting the results.

The method provides a means whereby a manager or consultant can gather a large amount of information in a very short period of time (typically, less than an hour). Because this method is based on anonymous and independent inputs, it can provide qualitatively different data than that normally obtained in a group setting using other idea-generation techniques. Used properly, it can provide deep penetration into problem areas, creative ideas for problem resolution, high-quality data for decision making, and ideas for productivity enhancement and organizational improvement.

When to use this technique:

- Use it when you want to get ideas from a large group of people;
- Use it when you do not have time or ability to discuss ideas and just want to collect people's thoughts;
- Use it when you want to engage an audience by giving them a sense of involvement.

Here are a few quick activities to engage in, learn and better access your creative thinking:

- Set aside time every day for creating some ideas.
- Set up brainstorming sessions on important issues and list all the ideas that come to you.
- Conceptualize a new project or program for your organization.

- Redesign your work spaces with different colors, designs or some new objects that spark creativity in you.
- Go online once or twice a week to see new trends in the market or industry that can help your business or organization to benefit.

Chapter 7: Key Takeaways:

Creativity is intelligence having fun, as Albert Einstein said once.

Creative thinking is not limited to only some limited set of people, such as artists, musicians or writers. It's the most essential skill in the modern business world. Surveys taken by top CEOs worldwide show that creativity as one of the top skills that they are looking for in their talent.

Creativity emerges by way of synaptic connections between the neurons in the brain.

Graham Wallas suggested four steps to creativity in his book, and Ned Herrmann further added two more steps to that. The **six steps to creativity** are:

1. Interest
2. Preparation
3. Incubation
4. Insights
5. Verification
6. Application

Ideas don't happen in a vacuum. Every new idea extends from the past and travels into the future through the present.

The Medici Effect states that in the intersection of different fields, disciplines and cultures, there's an abundance of extraordinary new ideas to be explored.

Asking questions is one of the most effective ways to generate new ideas. You can use the SCAMPER method to direct your questions in a specific manner that will trigger your mind to produce ideas in a targeted way.

You can follow a few other techniques to generate ideas like the **Magic Wand technique** or the **TLC (tempting, lacking, change)** technique.

Before we start nurturing ideas, there are multiple idea killers that can stop the flow of ideas. You need to **kill these idea killers** before they start germinating.

Just like you exercise your physical muscles, you need to exercise your idea muscles as well. **Setting up a daily idea quota** will force your brain to produce more ideas.

If you want to generate a large number of ideas from a group of people, you can follow the `**Crawford slip writing method.**

In Conclusion

****

*"The empires of the
future are empires of
the mind"*

~ Winston Churchill

You can only go so far with one thinking preference!

Often people become egoistical about their particular thinking preference, but that's a very limiting approach. If you were given a choice to run a car with 1,000 horsepower, would you still feel proud to drive a 500 horsepower car? Obviously, no!

Having read this book until the end, you now know that thinking with your full brain potential doesn't mean that you can't have any specific preference. While you should strive to strengthen your primary thinking preference, at the same time, you should nurture other thinking approaches to become a holistic thinker to make better decisions and solve complex problems faster.

To put it simply, you need to become situationally whole-brained so that you can handle different life situations that arise while dealing with people with a variety of different perspectives and thinking preference.

I sincerely hope that you have learned quite a few ways to develop different types of thinking preferences. The objective of putting all of this information together was two-fold. First, you'll further nurture your own preferred thinking style by learning effective techniques and second, when you learn about how the other thinking approaches work, you can implement the strategies necessary to develop other thinking preferences.

I also hope that you realize that merely by becoming aware of these multiple thinking approaches, you become a bit more flexible and willing understand a multitude of situations and a variety of people in a more holistic manner.

Lastly, if you want to improve your life in all aspects, you need to tap your mind's full potential and think flexibly and in a holistic manner.

Let me conclude with these powerful words from Albert Einstein:

"The world we have created is a product of our thinking; it cannot be changed without changing our thinking."

I wish you nothing but great success in your endeavors through the limitless power of your brain.

Cheers!

May I ask you for a small favor?

At the outset, I want to give you a big thanks for taking out time to read this book. You could have chosen any other book, but you took mine, and I totally appreciate this.

I hope you got at least a few actionable insights that will have a positive impact on your day to day life.

Can I ask for 30 seconds more of your time?

I'd love if you could leave a review about the book. Reviews may not matter to big-name authors; but they're a tremendous help for authors like me, who don't have much following. They help me to grow my readership by encouraging folks to take a chance on my books.

To put it straight— **reviews are the life blood for any author.**

Please leave your review by clicking below link, it will directly lead you to book review page.

DIRECT REVIEW LINK FOR "THINK WITH FULL BRAIN"

It will just take less than a minute of your time, but will tremendously help me to reach out to more people, so please leave your review.

Thanks for your support to my work. And I'd love to see your review.

Full Book Summary

INTRODUCTION: KEY TAKEAWAYS

Our thinking preferences changes based on the cultural and geographical differences.

As per the studies described in this introduction, while Americans perceived people, places and situations more specifically and individually, the Japanese looked at the bigger picture, and they looked at people, places and things in the context of their surrounding objects and their interrelation with these objects.

Two types of thinking are **specific thinking or holistic thinking**, and these types of thinking are the result of two vastly different perspectives.

Thinking by **utilizing your brain's full potential offers multiple benefits**:

- A heightened level of awareness
- Increased entrepreneurial capabilities
- Faster progress in your career
- Better relationships with family and friends
- The development of multiple forms of intelligence

Thinking with full brain involves utilizing the full capacity of your brain as required in any given situation. The benefits of unleashing the full power of your cognitive abilities will help you to **improve your life in all areas, be they financial or relational, and heighten your overall happiness**.

CHAPTER 1: KEY TAKEAWAYS

Most people suffer from the misconception that our thinking abilities depend on our Intelligence Quotient (IQ). But in reality, IQ is a limited parameter of assessing cognitive functioning for academic and work success, but they are not complete.

The **general IQ Tests cover only logical-mathematical intelligences**, but there are multiple types of intelligence. Howard Gardner described **seven different types of intelligences** in his book (as listed below) that determine the success of any individual in different facets of one's life:

- Logical-mathematical
- Verbal-linguistic
- Spatial-mechanical
- Musical
- Bodily-kinesthetic
- Interpersonal-social
- Intrapersonal (self-knowledge)

There are many **tests to assess the level of your intelligence,** and one of them is the MIDAS test. You can also get a sense of your multiple intelligences through the 9-minute, 80-question test that was provided as a link in this chapter.

Finally, **thinking with full brain entails tapping into the multiple intelligences** of human beings instead of merely restricting your focus to logical or linguistic abilities.

CHAPTER 2: KEY TAKEAWAYS

Many different theories and research studies have been conducted about the brain's physical structure, but we can also examine the brain from an evolutionary perspective.

The **two-hemispherical left-right brain** concept was propounded by Robert Sperry and led him to win the Nobel Prize in medicine. While the left brain is more logical and rational, the right brain is more imaginative and instinctual.

In the 1960s, there was a study conducted by Paul Maclean; it looked at the brain from an evolutionary perspective and concluded that there are **three major brain structures** that have developed sequentially.

- Reptilian **(instinctual)** brain

- Mammalian or limbic (**emotional**) brain
- Primate or neocortex (**thinking**) brain

Regardless of whether we are looking at the physical structure or the evolutionary aspects of the brain, **thinking in the brain happens in a very complex and non-linear manner**.

Our brain is said to have 100 billion neurons, and all thinking is nothing but these different neurons firing with each other and making synaptic connections. These **synaptic connections form a neural pathway that determines our thinking preferences**.

CHAPTER 3: KEY TAKEAWAYS

Our **brain is a powerful network of neurons** that interact with each other across the brain. A specific type of thinking doesn't result from any specific part of the brain; each individual has different thinking preferences. The more you use a specific part of the brain, the more dominant that part becomes.

Ned Herrmann propounded the concept of the **Four Quadrants of Thinking Preference** and advocated the view that different people have different types of thinking preferences. Here are the four Quadrants:

- **Quadrant A: The Analyzer**. Logical thinking, analysis of facts, processing numbers
- **Quadrant B: The Organizer.** Planning approaches, organizing facts, detailed review
- **Quadrant C: The Personalizer**. Interpersonal, intuitive, expressive
- **Quadrant D: The Strategizer.** Imaginative, big-picture thinking, conceptualizing

People choose to think in a particular way due to their preference, and it doesn't mean that they don't have the ability to think in a different manner; **preference is not the same as competency.**

Because of the **Preference-praise loop**, when people get praised for good work done in their area of preference, they develop that specific thinking preference further.

Understanding the different thinking patterns will help you deal with people of different thinking preferences and can **make you a situationally holistic thinker**.

CHAPTER 4: KEY TAKEAWAYS

Logical thinkers **observe and analyze phenomena, reactions, and feedback, and then draw conclusions** based on that input. They can justify their strategies, actions, and decisions based on the facts they gather.

You can develop your logical thinking abilities by following the effective strategies listed below:

- Learn to **get rid of your confirmation bias** and become open-minded. Follow multi-perspective thinking and review the counter-argument for every assumption. Look at a variety of opposing views about any specific situation, as that will empower you to make fine distinctions and help you improve your rational thinking.

- Get an **outsider's perspective** in difficult situations. Learn how an outsider will observe any specific situation; follow the "Revolving Door Test".

- **Understand the Halo Effect**: Don't make your decisions based on incomplete information or just outer appearances.

- **Don't believe something because it sounds reasonable and because it's said by some person of authority**. Examine all assumptions critically on your own before arriving at any conclusions or decisions.

- **Avoid becoming trapped by the sunk cost fallacy**: Don't justify your past mistakes and don't continue to make the same ones merely because it is what you have done in the past. Learn from the past and move forward.

- **Learn a foreign language** to look at things from a different perspective and get rid of the emotional bias associated with your own language.

- **Exercise your mind** by using memory-recall techniques. Do brain trainings; switch up your routine activities and engage in healthy debates with individuals who have a different viewpoint than yours on any given topic.

CHAPTER 5: KEY TAKEAWAYS

An organized mode of thinking **enables you to make plans, create structures, and set up clear processes** for doing all the smaller steps necessary to carry out the desired action.

You can use the **4-step process to organize your thoughts.** Below are the four steps:

1. Document your thoughts.
2. Sort your thoughts.
3. Reframe your thoughts.
4. Prioritize your thoughts.

Following **mind-mapping techniques** helps you organize your thinking and enables you to holistically see the bigger picture. You can do mind mapping using simply a pen and paper, or you can use web applications or software to organize the scattered information in your brain, free your brain from clutter, and to perform a better analysis of the information that you have.

Both the compartmentalization and the prioritization of your thoughts are necessary for organized thinking. You can't organize any process or system unless you put them into different categories and assign timelines or deadlines to them. **The Eisenhower Matrix** is a great way to prioritize tasks into what needs to be done immediately, planned, delegated, or eliminated.

You need to **break the bigger information into small chunks**, as they are easier to memorize and handle. You can start more quickly with smaller chunks of activities, and it gives you a good starting point to base your future analysis on.

The way that you organize your workplace or desk directly affects your thinking approach. If your desk is cluttered, you will find it difficult to organize your thinking. A study proved that people who had organized desks were better able to focus more on their work and got better results.

In the age of technology, you can effectively **use various online tools and applications** to organize your thinking and ideas.

CHAPTER 6: KEY TAKEAWAYS

The act of thinking is not merely a rational or logical approach; you need to also nurture the emotional and instinctual side of your brain.

An interpersonal thinking approach **empowers you to connect with people more effectively** and get results faster. The formula for getting results is as follows:

The higher the level of connection, the less that communication is needed, and the better the results. **The lower the level of connection**, the more communication is needed, and the results are less than optimal.

The following techniques can be used for developing interpersonal thinking:

Follow **Hanlon's Razor**; don't see malice or bad intention in a situation that can be justified by some genuine lapses.

Active Listening: You can build trust with the other people by following active listening skills to demonstrate concern using non-verbal cues, brief verbal affirmations, or disclosing similar experiences.

Make curiosity as a habit to develop empathy. Withhold your judgment of any individual, and display curiosity about their behavior.

Widen your circle by meeting new people and more people so that you can understand their concerns. You should especially meet people from other cultural or socio-economic groups than yours.

Reading literary fiction heightens your level of empathy for others, and thus, it develops your interpersonal thinking abilities.

Challenge yourself to have deeper conversations with your colleagues. When you deeply engage in conversation with someone, you understand the underlying emotions and feelings of the other person. You come to know and understand the key drivers or motivators that affect the person's behavior.

CHAPTER 7: KEY TAKEAWAYS

Creativity is intelligence having fun, as Albert Einstein said once.

Creative thinking is not limited to only some limited set of people, such as artists, musicians or writers. It's the most essential skill in the modern business world. Surveys taken by top CEOs worldwide show that creativity as one of the top skills that they are looking for in their talent.

Creativity emerges by way of synaptic connections between the neurons in the brain.

Graham Wallas suggested four steps to creativity in his book, and Ned Herrmann further added two more steps to that. The **six steps to creativity** are:

1. Interest

2. Preparation
3. Incubation
4. Insights
5. Verification
6. Application

Ideas don't happen in a vacuum. Every new idea extends from the past and travels into the future through the present.

The Medici Effect states that in the intersection of different fields, disciplines and cultures, there's an abundance of extraordinary new ideas to be explored.

Asking questions is one of the most effective ways to generate new ideas. You can use the SCAMPER method to direct your questions in a specific manner that will trigger your mind to produce ideas in a targeted way.

You can follow a few other techniques to generate ideas like the **Magic Wand technique** or the **TLC (tempting, lacking, change)** technique.

Before we start nurturing ideas, there are multiple idea killers that can stop the flow of ideas. You need to **kill these idea killers** before they start germinating.

Just like you exercise your physical muscles, you need to exercise your idea muscles as well.

Setting up a daily idea quota will force your brain to produce more ideas.

If you want to generate a large number of ideas from a group of people, you can follow the `**Crawford slip writing method.**

Could you please leave a review on the book?

One last time!

I'd love if you could leave a review about the book. Reviews may not matter to big-name authors; but they're a tremendous help for authors like me, who don't have much following. They help me to grow my readership by encouraging folks to take a chance on my books.

To put it straight– **reviews are the life blood for any author.**

Please leave your review by clicking below link, it will directly lead you to book review page.

DIRECT REVIEW LINK FOR "THINK WITH FULL BRAIN"

It will just take less than a minute of yours, but will tremendously help me to reach out to more people, so please leave your review.

Thank you for supporting my work and I'd love to see your review on the book.

Preview of the book "Mindset Makeover"

Introduction

****

"If you change the way you look at things, the things you look at change."

~ Wayne Dyer

A Short Story: How a Mindset Shift Can Change the Trajectory of Life

There was a middle-aged man in a small town. He had all sorts of bad habits associated with his name. He was a chronic alcoholic; day and night didn't matter to him when it came to drinking. In his drunken state, he was always misbehaving with the people around him. Shouting, abusing, calling names, and any other terrible thing you can think of — he was all that.

All in all, his life was a bit more than a disaster, from a societal standard or any other. With such a state of affairs, doing a day job or working on his own was out of the question. When he ran out of all his saved money, he chose the route of begging — or if he got a chance, even stealing. He ended up being arrested by the police a number of times for creating a nuisance and committing petty crimes.

Unfortunately, he had two sons in their early teenage years. Sorry, but what else could one call these two children other than unfortunate; negative impressions were getting imprinted on their innocent minds at such an early age.

With the passage of time, the man did not improve; rather, his situation only worsened — deteriorating further with each passing day, week and month. He died after only a few years, leaving behind his two sons.

The elder son was a true follower and started living a life very much like his father's. Drinking, gambling, drugs, etc. — he got into all kinds of negative activities and pursuits. His circle of friends included thieves, smugglers and other sort of criminals, so he was always surrounded with negative associations. In fact, he started exceeding his role model (i.e., his father) and ended up getting arrested by the police and put in jail for some serious criminal offenses.

On the other hand, the younger son, with such a terrible family condition and no financial support, was obviously not in a position to continue his studies. But he didn't want to end up like his father or brother; he had a deep sense of commitment to live a better quality of life. So, he started working in the evenings at burger joints serving tables and was able to manage his school fees out of his meager earnings.

His complete dedication and focus very shortly earned him a good annual scholarship to sponsor his studies. He continued to maintain his focus and kept going on the right track. Eventually, he got a decent job offer to work in a blue-chip company. Not only that, but due to his traits of deep focus and commitment, in only a short period of time, he became part of senior management and was made responsible for operating a specific unit of the organization. Soon his success was creating a ripple effect, his reputation in the industry was spreading, and he was invited for an interview on a TV show.

The TV anchor asked him about his family background, childhood, and growth trajectory and the specific reasons behind his success. He told the whole story of his father — his many wrongdoings and abdicating of all family responsibilities. He also told about his brother following the footsteps of his father and spoiling his own life, when during all those years, this younger son was putting in hard work and building his career. The TV anchor became very curious as to how these two brothers from similar origins had such divergent trajectories in their lives. She wanted to interview the elder brother as well to understand the deeper reasons behind the path he had chosen.

So, the TV crew traveled to the jail to interview the elder son, who was serving a sentence for his crimes. The anchor asked him, "How did you come to end up here, in this shady prison, at this early stage of your life?" The elder son replied with a stony face, "What else could be the fate of a person whose father was a drunken, ill-behaved man, who had done nothing to improve the lives of his children?"

Immediately, the anchor turned the camera to the younger son and questioned him, "And how is it that you've become so successful despite your father being a chronic alcoholic, ill-behaved, and irresponsible man his whole life?"

The younger son replied with a deep sincerity, *"How can a person choose to destroy his life when he has seen first his father wasting his life and then his brother following in his father's very footsteps? I didn't want to waste my life, so I had no choice but to follow a different and better route to design my life."*

Short story, but a grand life message! Two persons facing the same life circumstances had alternate perception of life and prediction of their future entirely on two different extremes.

One thinks that life has presented the circumstances before him and he must live strictly within those circumstances. He thinks there is nothing he can do to change his lot in life, and **considers himself in a victim's position.**

Another person, by contrast, might question whether he is bound to live his life as per these unfavorable circumstances or if he indeed has a choice. Is he bound to live as a victim, or can he **choose to place himself in the driver's seat,** mapping his own course before him — an entirely marvelous way of living a dream life.

This story reminds me of a wonderful quote by Dan Brown, the bestselling author of *The Da Vinci Code*: ***"Sometimes a change of perspective is all it takes to see the light."***

Anyone can see the difference in approach adopted by both sons of the irresponsible father.

The key difference is in their MINDSET – the **manner in which you look at things** that come your way- **your perspective on the people and situation** around you, i.e., **the lens** your eyes see the world through.

This simple personal philosophy, or the way of looking at things, is the single most important factor that makes all the difference as to whether you live an average or mediocre life...

or leave a legacy behind.

You can be in any life situation or circumstance — it could be the worst of the worst situation — and, still, with a positive mindset, you can find a calmer version of yourself than you otherwise would.

Okay, now let's get out of the fictional world and put the spotlight on you.

You might be wondering: how can you get the best out of this story and eventually this book? You might be seeking to know about this mindset thing before you even think of upgrading it.

A one-liner statement, *"Mindset is a way of looking at things in a particular way,"* is simple to *say* intellectually, but it is really difficult to truly implement and get the maximum benefit out of it.

Some Relevant Questions:

You might be thinking about a few relevant and important questions like below:

- How are **our minds different from our mindset**?

- What is so **special about the mindsets of super-achievers**? And how do they acquire them?

- How is it possible to be in such a resourceful state of mind when you are

205

surrounded by negative people?

- Is such a growth-oriented mindset only for a limited number of people who are lucky enough to get it as a gift from God, or **can any human being access and attain a resourceful mindset?**

I know those reading this book are precisely the very people who want to enhance their quality of life. I don't know about your personal life situations. You might be struggling to reach even your minimum desired level of success and live a reasonable life, or you could be someone who has already achieved moderate success and wants to reach the next level of his journey.

You could progress to any stage of your life and still find successful people ahead of you, from whom you can learn. I sincerely believe and hope you do as well that the journey of progress never stops. There is always room to grow and more that can be achieved. That's the beauty of this life that makes everyone wake up each morning and start the day with a hope of doing, each day, better than the last.

Attaining any level of growth or progress in life requires a positive and open outlook that triggers initial actions and then further paves the way to an exciting journey. You need to upgrade your mindset to first perceive the outside world, people and situations, the way high-achievers do, before you start to take empowered action towards your most important goals.

And that's what this book is all about – to upgrade, redesign and finally create a whole new mindset that helps you thrive in this world.

What you can get by upgrading your mindset:

- You open up to learning new concepts that expedites your growth at a much faster pace.

- You start to view problems as challenges and opportunities to learn from and grow.

- You become mentally resilient and perseverant to bounce back from failure with more zeal and vigor.

- You start to take more risks and, therefore, increase the rate of your learning by the failures and successes that emanate from the results.

- People start to perceive you as trustworthy person who is deeply motivated to learn, grow and contribute.

- You attract the right quality of people and events in your life, as your behavior and attitude impel people towards you.

- You increase your probability of better career growth. You can get promoted faster or if a business owner, you will take more risks, learn faster and thus earn more.

- As you are willing to learn from every person or situation, you improve the quality of your relations with colleagues, friends and family.

- And the list continues...

What you will learn from this book?

The aim of this book is to radically shift your perspective so you will perceive this world differently.

Although the story in this introduction may be a piece of fiction, in the real-world, we all hear life-changing and empowering stories of people who didn't give up in adverse situations. Rather, they demonstrated how one can turn things around and make the best out of adverse situations, just with a different outlook on life. (In the next chapter, we will see many real-life instances.)

I personally believe that if you're in a position to read this book on an electronic device or you have bought it, you have access to the basic amenities of life like electricity and the internet. So your situation is not as bad as the younger son in the story. I can say with assurance say that if you have a paying job or run your own small business venture, you already are in the top 5% (or maybe 1%) of the population of the world. Some of you might doubt this; and for those readers, I urge you to verify it at www.globalrichlist.com.

After realizing that you are in top 1% of the world population in terms of income or wealth, you'll understand that if the younger son could face adverse conditions (or your real-life heroes) and turn around his life, **you yourself are capable of taking charge of your mindset and, eventually, your destiny.**

I pray to God that no one be forced to suffer the kind of life we saw in the story due to bad parenting. No one should struggle so hard in adversities to live a better life, but at the end of the day, no one can be sure of what life has to offer. Therefore, the best approach is **to see life as a school, teaching us practical lessons by posing challenges and obstacles.**

You can treat this book as a recipe for overcoming life's adversities and problems and turning them into a challenge and adventure, as a pathway to your dreams.

What I want for you is to wake up every morning wondering what life has to offer- not just wondering, but filled with the thrill and excitement of facing any challenges in life.

Just a quick example from my corporate job days. I had the privilege of working with a manager who had the habit of the seeing "goodness" in everything that came his way, even if it was a terrible situation. The only word I heard from him was **'beautiful'** in the face of any challenge.

I really loved that approach as it immediately would bring a smile to my face and I would simply gear up to face the situation head on.

Do you want to see your life as beautiful, whatever color it comes in?

Do you want to welcome life circumstances as they come and make the most out of them?

If yes, then get ready to embark on a wonderful journey.

Here Is What You Are Going To Learn In This Book

We will first of all start to align your self-image and self-talk. Before you conquer the outside wars, you need to win the battle inside your own head.

You can't stay at your physical home; nor can you stay within your mind and thoughts at all times. The universe is created in such a way that you have to go out and meet people and touch other lives or get touched by them. When you have to be around people, then why not design your life in such a way that every touch and connection enhances your quality of life.

We will talk about how to insulate your life from the negative influences of the outside world, and more specifically how to deal with the negative people around us (optional and mandatory negative partners).

Then we will work on designing your everyday life with great habits that support your journey towards building a growth mindset.

Once you have identified and created your own new inside world, mastered quality habits, surrounded yourself with the right set of people, then you will learn how to welcome life's challenges and turn around the quality of your life.

You will embrace mistakes and learn lessons from them. You will persist and persevere and take the necessary lessons this life has to offer.

--End of Preview--

Get your copy of the full book here >>>

Mindset   Makeover:
Understand the Neuroscience

of Mindset, Improve Self-Image, Master Routines for a Whole New Mind, & Reach your Full Human Potential

Other Books in Power-Up Your Brain Series

1. **Mind Hacking Secrets:** Overcome Self-Sabotaging Thinking, Improve Decision Making, Master Your Focus and Unlock Your Mind's Limitless Potential (Power-Up Your Brain Book 1)

2. **Intelligent Thinking:** Overcome Thinking Errors, Learn Advanced Techniques to Think Intelligently, Make Smarter Choices, and Become the Best Version of Yourself (Power-Up Your Brain Series Book 2)

3. **Think Out of The Box:** Generate Ideas on Demand, Improve Problem Solving, Make Better Decisions, and Start Thinking Your Way to the Top (Power-Up Your Brain Series Book 3)

Made in the USA
Monee, IL
26 February 2020